FOUNDATIONS OF DEMOCRACY:

Authority, Privacy, Responsibility, and Justice

Law in a Free Society Series

Middle School and Above

Student Text

Center for Civic Education
5146 Douglas Fir Road • Calabasas, CA 91302 • (818) 591-9321

Cover:
Construction of the Treasury Building, September 16, 1861 (Library of Congress Photo)

The first edition of this text was developed with the support of a grant from the National Endowment for the Humanities.

This new and revised edition has been prepared under Grant #85-JS-CX-0009 from the Office of Juvenile Justice and Delinquency Prevention, Office of Justice Programs, U.S. Department of Justice.

Points of view or opinions in this document are those of the author and do not necessarily represent the official position or policies of the U.S. Department of Justice.

ISBN 0-89818-150-X

Summary of Contents

Introduction

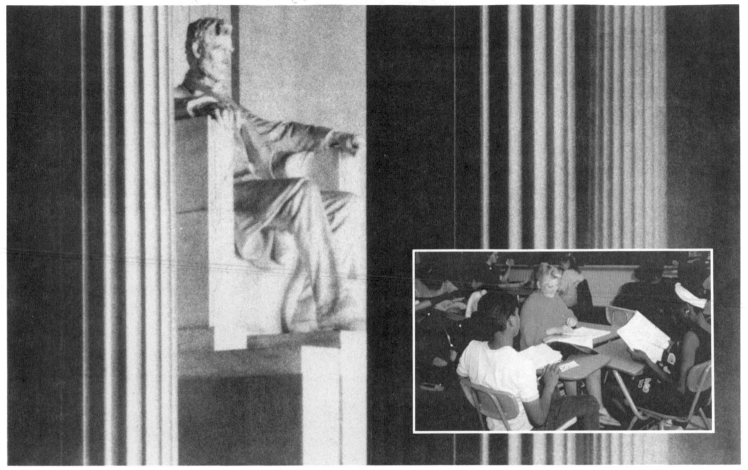

Foundations of Democracy introduces you to four ideas which are basic to our constitutional form of government: **authority, privacy, responsibility, and justice**. You will learn about these ideas and see how important they can be.

Authority, privacy, responsibility, and justice are not the only ideas that are important in understanding the foundations of our government. But these ideas will help you understand important differences between a constitutional democracy and a society which is not free.

You will learn that there are costs or burdens that we must bear in order to preserve the values on which our nation was founded. You will learn that there are many situations in which hard choices need to be made between competing values and interests.

You will be challenged to discuss and debate situations involving the use of authority and the protection of privacy. You will be asked to decide how responsibilities should be fulfilled and how justice could be achieved in a number of situations.

You will learn different approaches and ideas, which we call "intellectual tools," to evaluate these situations. Intellectual tools help you think clearly about issues of authority, privacy, responsibility, and justice. They help you develop your own positions, and support your positions with reasons.

The knowledge and skills you gain will help you in almost any kind of situation you face in your day-to-day life. And by thinking for yourself, reaching your own conclusions, and defending your positions, you can be a more effective and active citizen in a free society.

AUTHORITY
Table of Contents

Introduction

Thomas Jefferson (1743–1826), author of the Declaration of Independence

"We hold these Truths to be self-evident, that... Governments are instituted among Men, deriving their just Powers from the Consent of the Governed..."

This quotation from the Declaration of Independence contains one of our nation's most basic ideas about government. We, the people, give our representatives the power and right—the authority—to govern us. We have given government the right to make and enforce laws, and we agree to obey these laws.

We, as citizens, have the right to control how our government uses the authority we have given to

it. We exercise this control by voting and by participating in other types of political activity. Courts ensure that government uses its authority lawfully and according to the Constitution.

As citizens in a free society, all of us have the responsibility to deal intelligently with issues of authority. We need to understand authority and make informed decisions about its use.

This study of authority should help you gain a greater understanding of its purposes and uses. It also should give you a greater ability to deal effectively with issues of authority as they arise in your daily life as a citizen in a free society.

Unit One: What Is Authority?

What examples of authority do these pictures illustrate?

Purpose of Unit

This unit introduces you to the subject of authority. You probably know quite a bit about authority from your own experiences. You see it in action every day. In fact, you have been involved with authority in one way or another since you were born. We all have.

When you talk about laws and other rules, you are talking about one kind of authority. When you wonder whether someone has the right to tell you what to do or what not to do, you are thinking about authority. Authority has to do with laws and other rules and with people who sometimes have the right to tell others what to do.

When does someone have the right to tell you what to do? Do your parents have the right to tell you when you have to be home? Do state officials have a right to say you can't drive a car until you are sixteen? Do the police have the right to make you obey a law you believe is wrong?

These questions all involve authority. And questions of authority are often difficult. Some of the greatest minds in history have tried to figure out exactly what it is, why it is necessary, and how it should be used. In the lessons that follow, you will have an opportunity to consider these questions. To start, we must ask, "What is authority?"

LESSON 1

What Is the Difference Between Authority and Power Without Authority?

Purpose of Lesson

This lesson explains the definition of authority that will be used in this course of study. It also explains the difference between authority and power without authority.

Terms to Know

power
authority
customs
principles of morality

Critical Thinking Exercise
IDENTIFYING THE DIFFERENCE BETWEEN POWER AND AUTHORITY

A Dangerous Ride

Crime on subways in some cities is a serious problem. Roving gangs sometimes threaten passengers, rob them and, in some cases, physically attack them.

Who in this picture has the right to use power?

In one incident, late in the evening, two teenagers dressed in gang colors boarded a subway. One of the teenagers pulled a gun from his jacket. He demanded money and jewelry from an elderly couple.

A police officer riding on the car drew his gun and approached the gang members. "Freeze! Drop your guns and keep your hands in the air!" He quickly arrested and handcuffed the gang members.

What do *you* think?

1. What is similar about the actions of the gang members and the actions of the police officer?

2. What is different about their actions?

3. Which people were using power? Which of them had the right to use power? Which do not? Explain your answers.

What are power and authority?

The story you have just read illustrates the difference between **power** and **authority**. The difference between these two ideas is important.

- **Power** is the ability to control or direct something or someone.

Sometimes people have the right to use power. Sometimes they do not. For example, if your classmates try to force you to do something you don't want to do, they may have the power to do so. They do not have the right. On the other hand, when police officers control traffic, they have both the power and the right to do so.

- **Authority** is **power** combined with the **right** to use that power.

The right to use power usually comes from **customs** (traditions), **laws**, and/or **principles of morality** (basic ideas about right and wrong). For example:

■ Your parents have the authority to punish you in a reasonable way for wrongdoing. They get the right to exercise this power from custom, from the law, and from principles of morality.

■ Your teacher has the authority to decide how to teach your class because the law gives him or her the right to exercise this power.

Where do teachers get their authority?

■ Congress has the authority to pass laws because the Constitution gives it the right to exercise this power and the people consent to be governed under the Constitution.

Critical Thinking Exercise
IDENTIFYING THE USE OF AUTHORITY AND THE USE OF POWER WITHOUT AUTHORITY

This exercise will provide you with practice in identifying the difference between using authority and using power without authority. Read the following nine situations and answer the questions that follow them. Be prepared to explain your answers to the class.

1. A jury decides Maggie Smith is guilty of robbery and the judge sentences her to prison.

2. While his parents are out and leave him in charge, Chris Matthews tells his younger brother not to touch his computer.

3. The referee ejects two players from the game for fighting.

4. For as long as Maria Lopez can remember, her father has led the family in saying grace before dinner.

5. Bob Washington, who is bigger than most of his friends, cuts in front of the line at the movie theater.

6. The principal takes a knife away from a student and then turns him over to the police.

What authority do school principals have?

7. The city council refuses to give permission to a group of students who want to use Washington Park for a protest rally.

8. Angry about increasing violence in their school, a group of students march into the principal's office. They refuse to leave unless she agrees to install metal detectors and to hire armed security guards to maintain order on school grounds.

9. Richard Lee tells his son he is grounded for a week because he broke curfew.

Examining the Situations

1. Which of these situations illustrate the use of authority? Why?

2. Which of these situations illustrate the use of power without authority? Why?

3. **What do *you* think?** Why is it important to know the difference between power and authority?

Using the Lesson

1. While you are studying authority, you should keep a notebook or journal. Begin by describing two real or imaginary situations. The first should be an example of the use of authority. The second should be an example of the use of power without authority. You may draw pictures or use words to describe the situation.

2. Read the newspaper or watch the news on television. Identify two articles or reports which illustrate the use of authority or the use of power without authority. Be prepared to explain to your classmates how these articles illustrate the concepts of power and authority.

LESSON 2

Why Do We Need Authority?

Purpose of Lesson

In this lesson you will learn some uses of authority. You will examine a situation in which there is no effective authority and identify problems which the lack of authority creates. When you have completed this lesson you should be able to explain how authority can be used to deal with these problems.

Terms to Know

benefits
costs

What might happen if there were no authority?

Think of all the rules you follow every day. Then think about all the people in authority who sometimes tell you what to do. It might seem to you that there are too many rules. There may even seem to be too many people in authority.

But have you ever wondered what might happen if there were no rules and no people in authority? What would happen if some people started causing trouble? What if jobs didn't get done that had to be done? Who would settle arguments or protect people's rights? Who would run the government? Would there even be a government?

What do *you* think?

Imagine that you wake up one morning and find there is no longer any authority. All rules, laws, police, courts, teachers, principals, and governments have disappeared.

1. What problems might arise?

2. How would you protect your rights?

3. Would you even have any rights?

Critical Thinking Exercise
IDENTIFYING USES OF AUTHORITY

The following is an excerpt from Mark Twain's *Roughing It,* a story about the Old West. Twain writes about a time when people often took the law into their own hands. As you read this excerpt, think about what problems arose because there was a lack of effective authority.

Roughing It

The devil seems to have again broken loose in our town. Pistols and guns explode and knives gleam in our streets as in early times. When there has been a long season of quiet, people are slow to wet their hands in blood; but once blood is spilled, cutting and shooting come easy.

Night before last Jack Williams was assassinated, and yesterday forenoon we had more bloody work, growing out of the killing of Williams, and on the same street in which he met his death. It appears that Tom Reeder, a friend of Williams, and George Gumbert were talking, at the meat market of the latter, about the killing of Williams the previous night, when Reeder said it was a most cowardly act to shoot a man in such a way, giving him "no show." [After some more arguing,] Gumbert drew a knife and stabbed Reeder, cutting him in two places in the back.

Reeder [was] taken into the office of Dr. Owens, where his wounds were properly dressed. [Being] considerably under the influence of liquor, Reeder did not feel his wounds as he otherwise would, and he got up and went into the street.

How can the absence of authority endanger lives, liberty, and property?

He went to the meat market and renewed his quarrel with Gumbert, threatening his life. After these threats Gumbert went off and procured a double-barreled shot gun. [He came back, and shot Reeder twice. The doctors examined him and said it was almost impossible for him to recover.]

At the time that this occurred, there were a great many persons on the street in the vicinity, and a number of them called out to Gumbert when they saw him raise his gun, to "hold on," and "don't shoot!"

After the shooting, the street was instantly crowded with inhabitants of that part of the town, some appearing much excited and laughing—declaring that it looked like the "good old times of '60."...It was whispered around that it was not all over yet—five or six more were to be killed before night.

Examining the Situation

1. What problems arose in the town because there was no effective authority?

2. **What do *you* think?** How might authority be used to deal with these problems?

a. Are there similar problems in our society owing to a lack of authority?

b. What might be done to solve them?

How can we use authority?

You have just read about what can happen when there is no effective authority. Life in the Old West, as Twain described it, sometimes was violent and dangerous. Authority can be used to protect our rights to life, liberty, and property.

- **Authority** can be used to **provide order and security** in people's lives. For example, air traffic controllers prevent accidents and provide safety for airplane passengers.

- **Authority** can be used to **manage conflict peacefully and fairly.** For example, umpires are used to referee baseball games and solve conflicts that may occur. Courts manage conflicts among people over property and other matters.

- **Authority** can be used to **protect important rights and freedoms.** For example: the First Amendment of the Constitution protects our freedom of expression and belief.

- **Authority** can be used to **ensure that benefits** (advantages) **and burdens** (disadvantages) **will be distributed fairly**. For example: laws ensure that all children have an opportunity to receive a free public education; parents may require each of their children to help with household chores.

Critical Thinking Exercise
IDENTIFYING PROBLEMS RELATED TO AUTHORITY

As you read this story, look for problems that call for the use of authority. Then answer the questions that follow.

A Problem at Pacific Central High

As Alicia Hampton sprinted across the finish line, the crowd went wild. She had just run the final leg of the girls' 400-meter relay race in record time.

That race had given Pacific Central High School enough points to win the first state track championship in which both boys and girls competed.

On the way back to Pacific Central High, a few members of the team noticed their coach staring out the window of the school bus. "What are you thinking about, Mrs. Reed?" one of them asked. "Why aren't you celebrating like everyone else?"

"I was just thinking about how different things were the year I started teaching at Pacific Central High," she answered. "We won the state championship that year, too. But the only girls on the field then were cheerleaders."

"Wasn't there a girls' track team in those days, Mrs. Reed?" someone else asked.

"Oh, there was one," she answered. "But we didn't get to go with the boys to the state championship. We were lucky if we could get enough parents to drive us over to Porterville for a meet. Girls' teams took a back seat to boys' teams in those days. There was hardly any money left in the budget for the girls' athletic program."

How can authority be used to ensure fairness?

"I was the girls' coach then. Unlike the boys' coach, I was only paid for teaching during school hours. I didn't get paid for coaching the teams after school. I was asked to volunteer for the job. Our team could only use the track after the boys had finished. Since we never knew exactly when that would be, we had to wait around a lot. We usually finished practicing after dark. That, combined with the hand-me-down equipment we had to use, led to many injuries.

By this time others were listening to the conversation. One of them asked, "Why did things change?"

"Congress passed a law. It requires schools that receive government money to give both boys and girls equal opportunities in all school programs. Most schools receive money from the federal government, so the law made things change. When people from the State Department of Education began checking the schools, the situation improved even more."

"Well, if what you say is true, why does the girls' basketball team only get to use the gym twice a week?" asked Alicia. "And why don't we have a gymnastic team? I know a lot of girls who would like to compete in that sport."

"I heard that girls' coaches don't get paid as much as boys' coaches," Bonnie added. "That doesn't seem fair."

"There's still room for improvement," Mrs. Reed said. "But at least we're catching up. Now let's celebrate. After all, we won the state championship!"

Examining the Situation

1. What problems occurred at Pacific Central High School several years ago?

2. How was authority used to deal with these problems?

3. What problems at Pacific Central High School still have not been solved?

4. **What do *you* think?**

   a. How might authority be used to deal with these problems?

   b. How can you work to promote changes in a situation like this one?

Using the Lesson

1. Write a story in your journal about a time in your life when there was no authority to deal with a particular situation. Explain how authority might have been helpful to you at that time. For example, have you seen authority used to stop a fight at your school? You may also wish to illustrate your story with a cartoon.

2. Read the newspaper for several days. Keep a list of problems you read about that happened because there was no effective authority. After you have finished your list, write a letter to the editor suggesting ways authority can be used to deal with one of these problems.

3. As you watch your favorite television programs, notice how authority is used to deal with problems that arise. Report what you observe to your class.

LESSON 3

Where Is Authority Found and How Is It Justified?

Purpose of Lesson

In this lesson you learn where authority is found and some common arguments made to justify authority. When you have finished the lesson, you should be able to identify examples of authority and explain different arguments about its sources and justification.

Terms to Know

roles
institutions
source of authority
consent
supreme being
divine right

Where is authority found?

Where is authority found? We can look around every day and find people who have the authority to govern us and the way we act. Parents, teachers, police officers, and government officials are just some of the people who have the authority to regulate our actions. We are also controlled or influenced by laws and other rules. Some of the most common places we can find authority include the following:

- **Roles.** Certain **roles** (jobs or positions) carry with them the authority to regulate or control people's behavior, no matter which persons are in these roles. For example: anyone filling the role of a police officer has the authority to require people to obey traffic laws.

- **Institutions.** Groups of people, working together in certain **institutions**, or established organizations, also have the

authority to control or influence others. For example: your state legislature is an institution that has the authority to pass laws which people must obey.

What authority does Congress have?

- **Laws and other rules. Laws** and **rules** which we are obligated to follow have authority. For example: when you obey a law requiring you to attend school, you are recognizing the authority of the law.

- **Customs.** Customs or traditions often become so well established they may be said to have authority. For example: when you follow the practice, "first come, first served," you are recognizing the authority of a well established custom. It is a sign of the authority of this custom that, if you served someone at the back of the line instead of the person in the front, there probably would be loud complaints.

- **Moral principles**. Moral principles—basic ideas about right and wrong—have great influence or force in governing our behavior. Most people do what is right most of the time. Some do so mainly because they do not want to be punished for doing wrong. However, many people do what is right because they believe they should. For example: most people usually try to be fair and kind to others.

Would you steal something if you thought you wouldn't get caught?

Critical Thinking Exercise
FINDING YOUR OWN EXAMPLES OF AUTHORITY

Work with a study partner. Think of examples of authority you have dealt with since you woke up this morning. List a role, an institution, a law or rule, a custom, and a moral principle you dealt with today that has authority. Be prepared to discuss your examples with your class.

Where does authority come from?

We have seen that authority may be found in a number of places. The right to regulate or control our behavior may be held by people in certain roles, and by institutions, laws, customs, and moral principles. But where does that **right** come from? What is the source of the right? For example: where does the police officer get the right to tell us what to do? Where does Congress get the right to pass laws we must obey? In short, what is the **source of authority**?

Sometimes the source of authority for a rule or a position may be traced back through a number of steps. For example: the authority of a teacher to maintain order in the class can be traced back to the principal in charge of the school, who hired the teacher, to the superintendent who appointed the principal, and to the board of education which appointed the superintendent. From here it can be traced back to the state board of education, and to the laws that gave it the authority to make regulations about how schools should be run. Finally, authority can be traced to the state legislature which made the laws, and to the state constitution which established the state legislature.

Can you trace the sources of a teacher's authority?

Eventually, however, we can ask, "What is the ultimate or final source of authority?" for the government, or for customs and moral principles.

Depending on the answers, we may conclude that claims to authority are justified or unjustified. That is, examining the source of authority for a government, a custom, or a moral principle can help us decide whether or not we ought to obey it. For example: the ultimate authority of some customs may be simply that they have been followed for so long they are accepted without thought. If these customs are not supported by any good reason, you might decide not to follow them.

What arguments are made to justify the authority of rulers and governments?

Following are the most common arguments that have been used to justify the authority of rulers and governments.

- **Right given by a supreme being.** Rulers have often claimed their authority comes from a **supreme being** (a god). For example: kings and queens have often said they rule by **divine right**; that is, they claim to get their authority from God.

- **Right inherited by birth.** Some rulers have said they inherited their authority from their ancestors, who ruled before them.

How have kings justified their authority?

King George III of England (1760–1820)

- **Right justified by superior knowledge.** Some people have argued that those with superior knowledge should have the right to rule.

- **Right given by the consent of the governed.** Many governments today claim their authority comes from the people, who **consent** or agree to be governed by their elected representatives.

Why is it important to know the source of authority?

We need to know the source of people's authority in order to determine if they have the right to do what they are doing. If we know, for example, that the Constitution gives certain powers to Congress, we can look at the Constitution to judge whether a law passed by Congress is within the limits of its authority. We can also ask: What is the source of the Constitution's authority? In our government, the authority of the Constitution comes from the consent of the people.

People have different ideas about what should be considered to be a source of authority. They also may differ on which sources of authority should be considered more important or higher than others. To discuss such questions, it is necessary to identify and evaluate different sources of authority.

Critical Thinking Exercise
IDENTIFYING SOURCES OF AUTHORITY

The following selection deals with different sources of authority. Your class should be divided into small groups to complete this exercise. Each group should read the selection on the next page, *Regina v. Amah, Avinga and Nangmalik*, and discuss the questions that follow. Choose someone to note your answers and a spokesperson to report the group's opinions to the class.

Regina v. Amah, Avinga and Nangmalik

In the 1960s, Canadian courts had to rule on Inuit (Eskimo) customs which conflicted with the laws of the state.

In traditional Inuit camps, food was often scarce. In especially bad times, some people starved to death. Sometimes old people who felt they had become a burden on others chose to end their own lives. If assistance was required, another family member was asked to help. Respect for one's elders demanded that a person help in the suicide attempt.

Under Canadian law, it was illegal to aid in a suicide attempt. In 1963, a trial was held involving three Inuit charged with helping an elder commit suicide.

The Northwest Territories Supreme Court found all three men guilty. According to Canadian law, the penalty was up to fourteen years in prison. The court, however, also recognized the importance of the Inuit custom which demanded that relatives help an old person commit suicide. Instead of being sentenced to prison, the three men were allowed to return to their camp.

Examining the Situation

1. What was the source of authority for the actions of the Inuit? For the decision of the court?

2. How did the court deal with the conflict between two different sources of authority?

3. **What do *you* think?** How does this case illustrate the importance of identifying different sources of authority?

Using the Lesson

1. Consider the authority of a police officer who gives someone a ticket for speeding. Draw a chart that traces the authority of the officer back to its ultimate source.

2. Write an editorial defending or opposing the decision of the Canadian court in the case of *Regina v. Amah, Avinga and Nangmalik.*

Unit Two: How Can We Evaluate Rules and Laws, and Candidates for Positions of Authority?

How should we choose people for positions of authority?

Purpose of Unit

People in positions of authority have the right to control or influence our lives in many ways. In our country, we, the people, have the right to select those who serve in positions of authority in our government. Because we give these people power and responsibility, it is important that we choose them with great care.

Since we are also governed by rules and laws, it is equally important to be able to evaluate them to see which rules and laws are good and which should be changed or eliminated.

In this unit, you will learn some **intellectual tools** —specific sets of questions to ask, or things to consider—which are useful in selecting people for positions of authority and in evaluating rules and laws.

LESSON 4

How Should We Choose People for Positions of Authority?

Purpose of Lesson

This lesson introduces you to a set of intellectual tools which are useful in selecting people to fill positions of authority. These tools also are useful in evaluating the qualifications of persons who are in such positions. When you have finished this lesson, you should be able to identify and explain the requirements of a position of authority. You also should be able to identify and explain the qualifications a person should have to fill the position.

Terms to Know

> position of authority
> qualifications
> duties
> powers
> limitations
> diligence

Why should we be careful in selecting people to fill positions of authority?

Every day our lives are influenced by people in **positions of authority**, that is, people whose role or job gives them authority to regulate or control some part of our lives. For example: elected officials and those who are hired to assist them are in positions of authority. We give a great deal of power to many of these people. People who are well qualified to exercise authority can make our lives easier and better. Unqualified people in positions of authority can make our lives difficult and unpleasant.

Different positions of authority call for people with different **qualifications**—knowledge, skills, talents, and characteristics. Someone who is well qualified to be a police officer might not be qualified to be a judge. A person qualified to be a judge might not make a good police officer. When selecting people for positions of authority, it is important to consider what qualifications they should have to do their jobs well.

You may have the opportunity to choose people for positions of authority. For example: in your school you might vote to elect someone for class president. When you are eighteen, you will have the right to vote to select people to serve in your government.

Let's begin this part of our study by examining the qualifications of two leaders who filled important positions of authority early in the history of our nation.

Critical Thinking Exercise
IDENTIFYING QUALIFICATIONS FOR LEADERSHIP

The following was adapted from *The Winning of the West* by Theodore Roosevelt, U.S. president and historian (1858–1919). In this selection, he writes about the explorers Meriwether Lewis (1774–1809) and William Clark (1770–1838). As you read this excerpt, think about the characteristics Lewis and Clark had that qualified them to lead an expedition to the West.

Lewis and Clark Expedition

Lewis and Clark were appointed by President Thomas Jefferson to lead an expedition through the Louisiana Territory. The United States had bought the territory from France in 1803. With

Why might it be important to select qualified people for positions of authority?

luck, they hoped to find a water route to the Pacific Ocean.

Most of the area which they would cover had never been visited by people from the eastern United States. Vast plains, Native American tribes, mountains, and many rivers stood between them and their goal. President Jefferson, who chose Lewis and Clark for the journey, wanted them not only to get to the Pacific and back safely, but also to write about what they saw along the way.

Lewis and Clark were very accurate observers. Rarely have other explorers described so well the physical features, the animals, and plants of a newly discovered land.

Of greater importance, the two young captains had the qualities necessary to lead an expedition through unknown lands. They kept good discipline among the crew. They punished any wrongdoers, but not severely. They did their share of the work, took the same risks, and suffered the same hardships as the other members of the expedition.

Lewis and Clark were liked and respected by their followers, who obeyed them with loyalty and cheerfulness. They showed respect and concern in dealing with the Native American tribes. Only people who were so brave and thoughtful could have led the party safely among the dangers that they met.

Examining the Situation

1. What were the responsibilities of Lewis and Clark?

2. What qualifications did Lewis and Clark have that helped them fulfill their responsibilities?

How should we choose someone for a position of authority?

In the last activity, you listed some responsibilities of a particular position of authority. You also identified some of the qualifications of Lewis and Clark that enabled them to do their job well.

Following are some **intellectual tools**—a specific set of questions to ask and ideas to consider—that are useful in deciding whether someone is qualified for a particular position. Review them to prepare for the next exercise.

1. What are the **duties, powers, privileges**, and **limitations** of the position?

   Before you can decide how well qualified a person is for a position, you must first consider what the position involves. To do this, examine the position and answer the following questions:

   ■ What are the **duties** or responsibilities of the position?

- What **powers** or abilities to exercise authority are given to the person filling the position?

- What **privileges** are given to the person filling the position?

- What **limitations** or restrictions are placed on the powers of the person in the position?

2. What **qualifications** should a person have to fill the position?

   Each position has different requirements. A person needs to have the qualifications necessary for the particular job. Depending on what the position is, some important qualifications might include the following:

   - special knowledge or skills
   - ability to be fair
   - honesty
   - intelligence
   - diligence (willingness to work hard)
   - reliability or dependability
   - courage
   - ability to work with others
   - respect for the rights and needs of others
   - commitment to important values and interests

3. What are the **strengths** and **weaknesses** of each candidate?

   Each candidate's strengths and weaknesses should be considered in terms of the qualifications required for the position.

4. Based on your answers to the first three questions, which candidate would best fill the position? Why?

   You should be able to explain the reasons for your choice.

Critical Thinking Exercise
IDENTIFYING QUALIFICATIONS REQUIRED FOR A POSITION OF AUTHORITY

The following activity will give you an opportunity to practice using the intellectual tools you have just studied. Imagine that you are a member of a student government committee. You are to recommend students to serve as judges on a student court. The judges will be responsible for holding hearings and recommending punishments for students accused of causing discipline problems at your school.

Working in small groups, complete the chart on the next page. In the left-hand column of the chart, read the description of the duties, powers, privileges, and limitations on power for the position of a student judge. In the right-hand column, list the qualifications you think a person should have to do the job well. The first blank is filled in to give you an idea of the type of answers you might give. Use a copy of the chart for your answers.

After all groups have completed the exercise, each group should report its findings and discuss them with the entire class.

Using the Lesson

1. Select a position of authority. Describe the position in your journal and list the qualifications a person should have to fill the position.

2. Think of an upcoming election in your area for city, state, or national office. Give a short talk to your class discussing the questions that you think voters should ask themselves about the qualifications of the candidates.

Duties, Powers, Privileges, and Limitations of the Position of Student Judge	Characteristics a Student Judge Should Have
Duties. A student judge has the duty to 1. listen to all evidence presented in the hearing,	To perform these duties, a student judge should be 1a. able to listen well 1b. open-minded
2. question the accused student and any other witnesses, and	
3. interpret and apply school rules.	
Powers. A student judge has the power to 1. require accused students to appear for a hearing,	To exercise these powers, a student judge should be
2. require witnesses to appear and testify,	
3. keep order in the hearing,	
4. remove unruly persons from hearings, and	
5. decide cases and make recommendations about discipline and punishments.	
Privileges. A student judge has the following privileges: 1. the right to be excused from some school responsibilities in order to perform the job of judge, and	To be trusted with these privileges, a student judge should be
2. the right to hold hearings in private without teachers or administrators present.	
Limitations. As limitations on his or her power, a student judge 1. must provide fair hearings according to the rules,	To comply with (stay within) these limitations, a student judge should be
2. may not unfairly favor one student over another,	
3. must make decisions on the basis of facts and school rules, and	
4. may not recommend unfair or unreasonable discipline or punishments.	

LESSON 5

Who Should Be Selected for This Position of Authority?

Purpose of Lesson

This lesson gives you an opportunity to use the intellectual tools you have just studied to decide which candidate is most qualified for a position of authority. When you have completed the lesson, you should be able to explain what considerations you used to justify the choices you made.

Term to Know

ordinances

Critical Thinking Exercise

CHOOSING CANDIDATES FOR PUBLIC OFFICE

In this exercise you will be responsible for choosing the mayor of an imaginary city, Jeffersonville. You must consider different candidates for the position.

Your class will role-play a television debate with the four candidates for mayor. The debate will be run by the Fair Politics League of Jeffersonville and will be open to members of the community.

To begin preparing for this activity, read the following description of Jeffersonville and the

What kind of mayor does Jeffersonville need?

position of mayor. Then follow the instructions on preparing for and conducting the debate. Finally, read the section on reaching a class decision and conduct a mock election for mayor.

Mayor for Jeffersonville

Jeffersonville is a medium-sized city. At the last census, the population was about 120,000. Located an hour's drive from the state capital and about two hours away from a large metropolitan area, Jeffersonville is considered by many people to be an ideal place to live.

The population in the city has become increasingly diverse during the last ten years. The mayor and city council have worked hard to maintain good community relations. So far the diversity of the population has not caused any major problems, although there have been minor incidents involving name-calling.

Jeffersonville has a strong and varied economy; there is no shortage of jobs. A number of national companies have offices and factories in the area. There is little local industry, however, and some people are concerned about the future growth of the city. What would happen if some of the national companies closed their local offices and factories? How would the people who lost their jobs find work in Jeffersonville?

Public schools are another potential problem for the city. More and more people have settled in Jeffersonville. The schools have become overcrowded. There is a great deal of public debate about whether to raise taxes to build new schools.

Some people have argued that as Jeffersonville grows, it is losing much of its charm. An increasing number of citizens talk of trying to limit the growth of the city. Opponents argue that this would be a form of discrimination because most of the newcomers represent minority groups.

As the people of Jeffersonville face the upcoming election, they are concerned with the future of their city. The new mayor will have to decide a number of important issues.

The Position of Mayor

Duties and Powers. The mayor has the following duties and powers:

- heading the city administration
- presiding at city council meetings
- preparing the city budget
- planning for future city development
- recommending city ordinances (laws)
- appointing department heads
- hiring and firing city employees

Privileges. The mayor has the following privileges:

- an annual salary of $60,000
- use of a city-owned automobile

Limitations. The mayor has the following limitations:

- cannot hold another job while serving as mayor

- cannot violate the rights of individuals which are protected by the United States and state constitutions

Preparing for the Debate

Your class should be divided into small groups. One group will represent the Fair Politics League, which will ask questions and maintain order during the debate. Each of the other groups will represent one of the candidates for mayor.

The Fair Politics League

Your group will moderate the debate and ask the questions. You should study the candidate profiles carefully. You also should analyze the mayor's responsibilities and consider the qualifications necessary to fill that position successfully.

How can a public debate help you select the best-qualified candidate?

Your group should prepare questions to ask the candidates. You are trying to determine who is best qualified to be the mayor of Jeffersonville. It is your responsibility to give the community a chance to learn the candidates' positions on important issues.

Candidate Groups

Groups should read and discuss the candidate profiles that follow. List your own candidate's strengths and weakness and those of your opponents. Each group should choose one member to play the role of the candidate and help that person get ready for the debate. Prepare a short opening statement for your candidate to make. The candidate's statement should convince voters that he or she is the best person for the job. Each group also should help its candidate rehearse answers to questions he or she might be asked.

Other group members may assist the candidate during the debate.

Candidate Profiles

Robert "Bob" Burns. Owner of a thriving hardware chain, Bob has just finished his second term as president of the PTA. He is a well-known and popular businessman. Bob grew up in Jeffersonville, and his four children were educated in local schools. His wife, Janet, has been teaching English in the high school for almost 20 years. Bob has always been active in community life and is concerned with preserving the character of the city. He wants to maintain the prosperity of Jeffersonville but has doubts about encouraging new industry and additional growth.

Suzanne Winston. Suzanne is the youngest person to serve as president of the local lawyers association. A native of Jeffersonville, she went to the state university law school. After graduating she returned home to open her own office. After only ten years, she is highly successful and an expert on family law. She is divorced and has custody of her two children, who attend local schools. She has been an advocate of increased spending for education. Suzanne supports city growth, and wants to attract additional industry to Jeffersonville.

Jamie Tsing. An immigrant from China who has become a citizen, Jamie came to Jeffersonville ten years ago. Jamie has become fluent in English, gone to college, and established a successful business. Jamie also has become the leading spokesperson for the immigrant communities in Jeffersonville. Jamie has served two terms on the Community Relations Committee. Jamie also has tried to improve relations between the newcomers and the older residents of Jeffersonville. Jamie has recently married and has no children.

Instructions for Conducting the Debate

1. The chairperson of the Fair Politics League will moderate the debate.

2. Each candidate will have two minutes to make an opening statement.

3. League representatives will take turns asking questions. Candidates will be given thirty seconds to answer each question. Candidates should take turns answering first, second, and third.

4. A timekeeper should make sure that all candidates observe the time limits.

Reaching a Class Decision

After the debate, your class should conduct a mock election for mayor. The following questions should be considered when voting:

1. What are the duties, powers, privileges, and limitations of the position of mayor?

2. What qualifications should a person have to fill the position of mayor?

3. What are the strengths and weaknesses of each candidate?

4. Which candidate do you think is best qualified to be mayor? Why?

Discussing the Election

Following the mock election, your class should discuss how useful the intellectual tools were in helping you decide how to vote.

Using the Lesson

1. How did the debate help you evaluate the candidates' qualifications for the position of mayor? In what other ways did the debate help you decide how to cast your vote? What are the advantages of public debates between candidates for public office? What are the disadvantages?

2. Invite a the mayor or someone from the mayor's staff to your class. Ask that person to describe the duties, powers, privileges, and limitations of the position of mayor, and to identify the qualifications the mayor needs to have. Are the qualifications the speaker mentions different from those your class identified? In what way?

LESSON 6

What Should Be Considered When Evaluating Rules?

Purpose of Lesson

Just as we need to decide how well-qualified a person is for a position of authority, we need also to evaluate the rules we are required to follow. Some people think that just because a rule or law exists, it must be good or serve a useful purpose. This is not always true. Rules and laws can have many things wrong with them.

This lesson introduces you to some intellectual tools useful in making and evaluating rules and laws. When you have completed the lesson, you should be able to use these tools to evaluate rules and suggest how they might be improved.

Terms to Know

criteria
characteristics

Critical Thinking Exercise
DEVELOPING CRITERIA FOR EVALUATING RULES

The following rules were supposed to help the people of Dry Gulch save water. Each of the rules contains at least one weakness. Thinking about how to correct these weaknesses will help you identify some **criteria** or standards for evaluating rules. Read the rules and then answer the questions that follow them.

1. Only those people who have lived in Dry Gulch for at least five years are permitted to water their lawns.

2. Residual water rights may not be abrogated unless specifically designated by superseding regulations.

3. Everyone must pay his or her water bill by the fifteenth day of each month.

4. Anyone who uses too much water will have to pay a fine.

5. The water commissioners can come into anyone's home whenever they want, day or night, to check for leaky faucets.

6. No one may use any water for any purpose during the next year.

What do *you* think?

Answer the following questions for each rule.

1. What is the weakness of the rule?

2. After you think about how to correct the weakness, complete the following sentence: "A good rule should...."

How can you decide what makes a good rule?

In the previous activity, you were asked to evaluate some rules and think about how to improve them. In doing so, you made a list of **characteristics** or features a good rule should have. Your list may have included the following characteristics, for example:

A good rule should be

- fair
- easy to understand
- well designed to achieve its purpose
- clear as to what is expected
- designed so that it doesn't interfere unnecessarily with other values such as privacy or freedom
- possible to follow

When you evaluate a rule or law it is useful to consider whether it has these characteristics. That is, asking whether a rule or a law has these characteristics is one of the intellectual tools you can use to evaluate the rule or the law. Other intellectual tools you can use to evaluate rules and laws are printed in the chart on page 27.

Critical Thinking Exercise
EVALUATING RULES

This activity will give you an opportunity to use the intellectual tools to evaluate a rule. Working in small groups, read the story below and answer the questions in the Intellectual Tool Chart that follows. Be prepared to share your answers with the class.

The School Locker Debate

What's a school without lockers? To many administrators and teachers, it's a quieter, safer place. Students get to class on time, hallways are less noisy, and there's one less place to hide things that are not permitted on school grounds.

In some school districts, the school boards have made a new rule—no lockers. Those that exist have been removed or bolted shut. Many new schools are being built without lockers. Principals of the locker-free schools are full of praise for the new rule.

Students at these schools are less enthusiastic. They complain of having to carry all their textbooks, gym clothes, notebooks, and other equipment—sometimes weighing as much as twenty-five pounds—around with them all day. Students also say they miss the sense of responsibility having a locker implies. "I feel like a baby. I might as well be back in elementary school," argued one seventh-grader. Others claim, "We want our rights! Students need their lockers!"

What would you think of a rule banning school lockers?

Using the Lesson

1. Imagine your school board has just announced that beginning next fall students will not be permitted to wear hats, caps, jackets, or shirts with names or designs of professional sport teams on them. Use the Intellectual Tool Chart to evaluate the proposed rule. Then write an article for your school paper stating your opinion on the proposed rule.

2. Think of a problem that exists at your school. Work with a group of classmates to develop a rule to help deal with that problem. Present your proposed rule to the class. Be prepared to answer questions from the class about the strengths and weaknesses of your proposed rule. After your presentation, your class should vote on whether to support the proposed rule.

Intellectual Tool Chart for Evaluating Rules and Laws

Questions	Answers
1. What is the rule to be evaluated?	
2. What is the purpose of the rule?	
3. Is a rule necessary or are there better ways to accomplish the same purpose?	
4. What might be the effects of the rule?	
5. What are the strengths and weaknesses of the rule? Is the rule ■ fair ■ easy to understand ■ well designed to achieve its purpose ■ clear as to what is expected ■ designed so that it doesn't interfere unnecessarily with other values such as privacy or freedom ■ possible to follow	
6. **What do *you* think?** Should the rule be kept as it is, changed, or eliminated? Why?	

LESSON 7

How Might You Evaluate and Improve a Law?

Purpose of Lesson

This lesson will give you an opportunity to use the intellectual tools you have studied to evaluate the First Amendment to the United States Constitution. When you have completed the lesson, you should be able to explain and defend the position you have taken on how the First Amendment should be written.

Terms to Know

Bill of Rights
free exercise of religion
assemble
petition
redress
grievance

What is the First Amendment?

Our Constitution is the supreme law of the land. The Framers who wrote the Constitution included certain protections for the rights of citizens. For example, the Constitution protects your right to a trial by jury. As originally written, however, the Constitution did not include the **Bill of Rights**—the first ten amendments to the Constitution, which contain important protections of individual rights.

Many people were concerned about the lack of a bill of rights. They thought a list of individual rights should be included in the Constitution. They believed this was necessary to protect the people from the possibility of unfair use of power by the government.

The early Americans' knowledge of history and their past experience with the British government gave them good reason to be worried. In England

Why did some people want to add a bill of rights to the Constitution?

and in the colonies, **free exercise of religion**—the right to hold religious services and worship—was not guaranteed. People had been treated unfairly for practicing religious beliefs not favored by the government.

Freedom of speech and freedom of the press also were not guaranteed. People in positions of authority also had imprisoned those who spoke out against them. They had destroyed newspapers and other publications that criticized them. Citizens had been arrested and put in prison for **assembling** (gathering together or meeting) to practice their religion or to discuss political affairs. Others had been imprisoned for **petitioning** (asking) the government for a **redress** (correction) of **grievances** (wrongs).

People who were critical of the proposed constitution feared such things could happen again. They insisted that a bill of rights be added to the constitution to protect their rights from violation by government officials who might use their authority unfairly.

Imagine that you are a member of the first Congress of the United States. You have the right to suggest amendments to the Constitution and to evaluate those suggested by others. Some members of Congress have just suggested the amendment in the next section. What do you think of it?

Critical Thinking Exercise
EVALUATING A CONSTITUTIONAL AMENDMENT

Work with a study partner. Read the First Amendment to the Constitution. Use the questions which follow to help you evaluate the amendment.

Amendment I
Freedom of Religion and Expression

Congress shall make no law respecting an establishment of religion, or prohibiting the free exercise thereof; or abridging the freedom of speech, or of the press, or the right of the people peaceably to assemble, and to petition the Government for a redress of grievances.

Examining an Amendment

1. What are the purposes of the amendment?

2. Is the amendment necessary, or can the purposes be accomplished in better ways?

3. What might be the effects of the amendment?

4. What do you think are the strengths and weaknesses of the amendment? Is it

   ■ fair

   ■ easy to understand

   ■ well designed to achieve its purpose

   ■ clear as to what is expected

   ■ designed so that it doesn't interfere unnecessarily with other values, such as privacy and freedom

   ■ possible to follow

5. Do you think the amendment should be kept as it is, changed, or eliminated? Why?

Critical Thinking Exercise
DEVELOPING AND DEBATING A CONSTITUTIONAL AMENDMENT

In this exercise your class will develop and debate alternative ways to write the First Amendment. Your class should be divided into three groups. Each group should be assigned one of the following freedoms and should write a proposed amendment to protect it.

   ■ Freedom of religion

   ■ Freedom of speech and of the press

   ■ Freedom to assemble and to petition the government to correct wrongs

Each group should select a chairperson to help lead discussions and someone to take notes. In writing the amendment, be sure to take into account what you have learned about how fair and reasonable laws should be written. Also, keep in mind that the amendment should

- limit the authority of government, so government cannot unreasonably or unfairly limit people's freedom, yet

- leave enough authority for government to place fair and reasonable limitations on people's freedom in order to make society better for all

After each group has written its proposed amendment, the class should conduct a debate.

What arguments can you make to support your amendment?

Conducting a Congressional Debate

1. The class should select a person to serve as speaker of the House who will chair the proceedings.

2. Each group will have three minutes to present its amendment to the House. Presentations should be organized around the following questions:

   a. What is the purpose of your amendment?

   b. Is the amendment necessary or are there better ways to achieve the same purpose?

   c. What do you think will be the effects of your amendment?

   d. What are the strengths and weaknesses of your amendment?

   e. Why do you think your amendment should be passed by Congress?

3. After each presentation, other members of Congress may question or criticize the amendment presented. Members of the group creating the amendment may respond to these questions.

4. Each group may change its amendment to win the support of other representatives. Groups also may work out a compromise amendment to try to win a majority of class votes.

5. After debate has been completed, the House should vote on the amendments before it. Class members should be able to explain why they voted for or against each proposed amendment.

6. Complete this activity by discussing how useful the intellectual tools you have studied are in evaluating rules and laws.

Using the Lesson

1. Did you agree with the results of the class vote? Why or why not? As a reporter, write an article describing your reaction to the House debate and vote. Discuss your views about what type of amendment would best protect individual freedoms.

2. Read Article V of the Constitution to see how amendments may be added to the Constitution. Report what you learn to the class.

Unit Three: What Are the Benefits and Costs of Using Authority?

What might be some benefits and costs of using authority?

Purpose of Unit

Every use of authority has certain consequences. Some of these consequences are **benefits** (advantages); some are **costs** (disadvantages). Knowing the possible consequences of the use of authority helps us make decisions about issues of authority. For example, if you are trying to decide whether to vote for a certain law, you need to think about what the benefits and costs of the law might be.

In this unit, you will identify some common consequences of the use of authority. You will classify these consequences as either benefits or costs. You also will learn that different people may have different opinions about whether the benefits of the use of authority in a particular situation outweigh the costs.

LESSON 8

What Are Some Consequences of Using Authority?

Purpose of Lesson

In this lesson, you will identify consequences of the use of authority. You will classify these consequences as benefits or costs. When you have completed the lesson, you should be able to explain some common benefits and costs of authority and be able to use these ideas in evaluating and taking positions on issues of authority.

Terms to Know

predictability
efficiency
accountability
vigilance
inaccessibility
economic costs
incompetence

Critical Thinking Exercise
IDENTIFYING AND CLASSIFYING
CONSEQUENCES OF AUTHORITY

This activity gives you the opportunity to identify some consequences of exercising authority. You then classify those consequences as benefits or costs.

Your class should be divided into small groups. Each group should be assigned one of the situations described and answer the questions that follow. Each group should then share its answers with the rest of the class.

1. To reduce the number of automobile accidents among teenage drivers, the state legislature passed a law changing the age for getting a driver's license to twenty-one.

2. Suppose there has been a sharp increase in shoplifting by students in the area near your school. In answer to complaints from local store owners, your principal made a new rule that students could not leave the school grounds during lunch time.

3. To control pollution, the City Council passed a new law—the owners of any factory found guilty of dumping waste into the river would have to pay a large fine.

4. The state was suffering from its fourth year of drought. To deal with the water shortage, the legislature passed a law regulating the

use of water. Among other restrictions, residents could only water their lawns once a week.

What do *you* think?

1. What might be the consequences of using authority in this situation?

2. Which of these consequences do you think are benefits? Why?

3. Which of these consequences do you think are costs? Why?

Critical Thinking Exercise
EXAMINING COMMON BENEFITS AND COSTS OF AUTHORITY

The following are some of the most common benefits and costs of authority. Read each one and the examples that illustrate it. Then work with at least one other person to write an example from your own experience that illustrates each benefit and cost.

Benefits

1. **Security.** Authority can be used to make people feel more secure by providing order and **predictability** (knowledge of what to expect). For example:

- Traffic laws may make driving and walking across streets orderly and predictable, and help people feel safe and secure.

- Police patrolling your neighborhood may reduce or prevent crime and make neighborhoods safer and more secure.

2. **Fairness.** Authority can be used to promote fairness. For example:

- Laws require employers not to discriminate unfairly against their employees on the basis of age, sex, religion, ethnic or racial background, or physical handicap.

- Judges ensure that fair procedures are used in courts when people are accused of crimes.

- The Constitution prohibits cruel punishments from being imposed on people convicted of crimes.

3. **Freedom and other rights.** Authority can be used to protect individual freedom and other rights. For example:

   - The First Amendment protects your rights to freedom of religion and freedom of expression from unfair and unreasonable interference by government.

   - Police must respect your rights to liberty and privacy; they are not permitted to arrest or search you without good reason.

4. **Efficiency (wise use of resources).** People in authority can promote efficiency by assigning responsibility for jobs to qualified people. For example:

   - A general may assign different responsibilities to different soldiers in order to wage war effectively.

   - The principal of your school may assign teachers to different classes according to the grades and subjects they are best at teaching.

5. **Provision of essential services.** Authority can be used to provide essential services. For example:

   - We authorize the postal service to deliver the mail.

   - We give courts and law-enforcement agencies the authority to maintain law and order.

6. **Improved quality of life.** Authority can be used to protect and improve the way people live. For example:

   - Laws can protect you against dangerous foods and drugs, unclean water, impure air, and dangerous wastes.

   - Anti-noise and zoning laws can contribute to your enjoyment of your home.

Costs

1. **Misuse of power.** People in authority might misuse their positions and power. For example:

   - Members of a city government might use their positions unfairly to favor friends or people who supported their election.

   - Police officers might unfairly and unreasonably arrest people or search their persons or homes.

2. **Need for vigilance (watchfulness).** When we give people authority, we have to take time and energy to make sure they fulfill their responsibilities properly. For example:

- Businesses hire managers and supervisors to make sure employees do their jobs.

- Citizens have the responsibility to stay informed about how government is performing its duties. Organized groups often spend time and money to keep track of the way governmental agencies use tax money, how they enforce laws against environmental pollution, or how police treat citizens suspected of crimes.

3. **Inaccessibility.** In the United States, many different people and institutions are given authority to fulfill different responsibilities. Because of the size and complexity of our government at local, state, and national levels, the right person or agency to speak to about a problem may be **inaccessible** (difficult to contact). For example:

- The president of the United States has so many problems to deal with he or she may not have time to listen to your concerns.

- A family needing afforable housing may have to visit many different government offices to get help.

- If you think your school system is not getting enough money you may not know who you should ask to solve the problem.

4. **Limitations on freedom and other rights.** Every use of authority involves some limit on freedom. For example:

- Your parents may assign you household chores that you do not want to do.

- Traffic laws may prevent you from driving as fast as you want to go.

5. **Economic or financial costs.** It costs money to support people and institutions in positions of authority such as those in your local, state, and national government. For example:

- People are taxed to pay the salaries of law enforcement officers, judges, and teachers.

- People pay taxes to support the armed forces and to pay for the resources needed to defend the country.

Which benefits and costs are most important?

Evaluating the benefits and costs of using authority is important. Before making decisions about laws or the acts of persons in positions of authority we need to decide which consequences of the use of authority are most important to us. Are the benefits more important than the costs? Or do we feel the costs outweigh the benefits?

People may disagree about these questions. For example, suppose there has been a sharp increase in shoplifting near your school. Suppose some store owners persuade your principal to impose a rule that forbids students to leave the school grounds during lunch time. All people would agree that one cost of the rule would be its limitation of students' freedom. A benefit might be decreased shoplifting by students. Some people might think that the benefit of decreased shoplifting is more important than the cost of limiting students' freedom. Others might not agree. As you can see, it is important to consider different points of view when examining the benefits and costs of authority.

Critical Thinking Exercise
CONSIDERING BENEFITS AND COSTS IN TAKING POSITIONS ON ISSUES OF AUTHORITY

Assume that your state legislature is considering a law to encourage students to remain in high school until graduation. One part of the proposed law says that if students drop out of school, they lose their drivers' licenses.

Work in small groups. Each group should represent one of the following organizations:

- Committee to Protect Students' Rights
- Police Department
- Parent-Teacher Association
- Jobs for Youth Employment Agency

Develop a position on this proposed law from the point of view of your organization. Use the questions which follow to help you state your position. Then, be prepared to present your position and discuss it with your class.

Questions to Consider

1. What position might your group take on the proposed law?

2. What benefits and costs did your group identify?

3. What interests influenced your group's evaluation of the benefits and costs?

Using the Lesson

1. **What do *you* think?** What position would you take on a law which would take driver's licenses away from students who drop out of school? Write a letter to the editor defending your position in terms of the benefits and costs of the proposed law.

2. Draft a law that you think will encourage young people to graduate from high school. List the benefits and costs of the law and explain why you would support it.

3. What are some rules in your family? Do you have to be home by a certain time? Are there chores you have to do? Are you allowed to watch television before you finish your homework? Pick two or three of the rules at your house and, in your journal, describe the benefits and costs of each.

LESSON 9

How Would You Evaluate the Benefits and Costs of a School Dress Code?

Purpose of Lesson

In this lesson, you have the opportunity to think further about the benefits and costs of using authority. You will participate in a mock school-board hearing to consider the question of dress codes in the public schools. When you have completed the lesson, you should be able to explain the usefulness of considering benefits and costs in making decisions about authority.

Read the following selection and then work with a study partner to answer the questions that follow.

The School Unifom Debate

The city of Springville and its suburbs have more than a million people. The school district serves the entire metropolitan area. During the last few years, there has been a sharp increase in incidents of violence and theft on school campuses.

The Springville Unified School District has been considering ways to make campuses safer and improve discipline. A dress code has been proposed. It would require students to wear school uniforms. This proposal has been controversial. Some principals, teachers, parents, and students support the proposal. They argue that school uniforms would

- eliminate the problem of theft of students' clothes, shoes, and jewelry
- prevent violence caused by the wearing of gang colors
- eliminate peer pressure to wear "name brand" clothes
- prevent students from being ridiculed or laughed at for the way they dress
- enable students to concentrate more on their studies and less on their appearance

On the other hand, many students and their parents resent the idea of anyone telling them what to wear. They find the idea of a dress code

What might be the benefits and costs of a school dress code?

What arguments could you make for and against a school dress code?

which requires school uniforms completely unacceptable. "This is a free country," they say. "No one has the right to make me wear a uniform or cut my hair. The way I look is who I am."

What do *you* think?

1. What might be the consequences of the school board deciding to require students to wear uniforms in the Springville public schools?

2. Which of these consequences would be benefits?

3. Which of these consequences would be costs?

Critical Thinking Exercise
IDENTIFYING AND WEIGHING BENEFITS AND COSTS

The Springville Unified School District is conducting a hearing on the issue of dress codes in the public schools. The school board has opened the hearing to any group which wishes to testify.

Your class should be divided into six groups. Each group will represent one of the following:

- School Board
- Students and Parents for School Uniforms
- Students and Parents for Free Choice
- Springville Teachers Union
- Protect Our Rights Association
- Association of Springville School Principals

1. The school board should select a chairperson to conduct the hearing. Members of the school board should prepare questions to ask at the hearing.

2. To prepare for their testimony, the other groups should consider the benefits and costs of the proposed dress code. Each group should select someone to take notes of the discussion and a spokesperson to present the group's views.

3. Each group, except the school board, should prepare a brief presentation supporting or opposing the dress code proposal on the basis of the benefits and costs the group has identified. Group members who are not spokespersons should be prepared to answer the school board's questions.

Conducting the Hearing

1. Each group will have three minutes to make its presentation. Members of the school board may interrupt the presentation only to clarify any points made.

2. After each group has finished its presentation, school board members may ask questions. These questions should be answered by all group members, not just the person making the presentation.

3. When the hearing is over, members of the school board should discuss the points raised by each group. After considering the benefits and costs involved, the school board should decide whether or not to adopt a dress code requiring school uniforms in the Springville Unified School District.

4. The chairperson of the school board should announce and explain the reasons for the board's decision.

Discussing the Hearing

Afterwards, the class as a whole should discuss the following questions:

- What benefits and costs did the board decide were most important?
- What else did the board consider in making its decision?
- Do you agree with the board's decision? Explain.

Using the Lesson

1. Write a letter to the student body supporting or opposing the position taken by the school board on the issue of dress codes in Springville.

2. Propose an alternative to deal with the problems that exist in the Springville schools. Write an essay in your notebook or journal explaining the benefits and costs of the solution you propose.

3. Find an example on television or from the newspaper that shows an exercise of authority. In your journal, make a list of consequences of this exercise of authority. Label each consequence you list as either a benefit or a cost. Evaluate these benefits and costs. Then decide whether you support or oppose this exercise of authority. Explain your position in your journal.

Unit Four: What Should Be the Scope and Limits of Authority?

Book burning in Nazi Germany (1933) Inset: Adolf Hitler (1889–1945)

Purpose of Unit

Some of the most important issues we face as citizens involve questions about the scope (extent) and limits (boundaries) of authority. Is a particular position of authority well designed? Does it give too much or too little power to the person occupying the position?

In this unit, you will learn some intellectual tools to use in evaluating positions and institutions which have authority. These tools will help you decide whether the duties, powers, privileges, and limitations of a position or an institution have been well planned, or if they need to be changed. You also will have the opportunity to use these tools to design a position of authority.

LESSON 10

What Should You Consider in Evaluating a Position of Authority?

Purpose of Lesson

This lesson introduces you to a set of intellectual tools useful in evaluating positions of authority and institutions which have authority. When you have completed the lesson, you should be able to use these tools in evaluating and suggesting improvements for positions of authority.

Why is it important to be able to evaluate positions of authority?

You have learned how much people in positions of authority can affect your life. In the United States and in other countries around the world, government officials and institutions have great powers and responsibilities.

To preserve the freedom of our society, we need to be able to evaluate how well positions and institutions of authority are designed. People in positions of authority should be given enough power to do their jobs. But we must place effective limits on their powers in order to protect our rights. The following exercise will give you some useful ideas for evaluating positions of authority.

Critical Thinking Exercise
IDENTIFYING WEAKNESSES IN POSITIONS OF AUTHORITY

Each situation in the next section contains a position of authority that has a particular weakness. Read the situations and then, for each one, answer the questions that follow.

WHAT'S WRONG HERE?

1. In the State of Ukiah, the governor had to make all the laws, deliver the mail, sweep the streets, patrol for stray animals, make decisions in all criminal trials, and run the television station.

2. In the State of Parthenia, all members of the legislature were appointed for life. Once they were appointed, there was no way to remove them from office.

3. The manager of a nightclub hired Max Hardin. She told him his job was to remove customers who did not behave properly. She said he could use as much force as he wanted. Max injured many people.

4. In the years before the Russian Revolution, Czar Nicholas II had little contact with his people. They had no right to meet with him to express their concerns. He relied entirely on what his advisors told him. By the time he realized his people's unhappiness, it was too late.

People burning the Czar's coats of arms during the Russian Revolution (1917).

5. The city of Brookton hired six animal control officers to round up stray animals. But the city didn't give the officers any trucks, nets or leashes.

6. In England in the 1600s, the Star Chamber investigated crimes against the king. The judges used torture to get confessions from persons accused of crimes.

What do *you* think?

1. What position of authority is involved in each situation?

2. What is the purpose of the position?

3. What weakness or problem do you think the position has?

4. What does this weakness suggest about a well-designed position of authority?

How can you evaluate a position of authority?

As you can see, positions of authority need to be properly planned. For example, people in a position of authority must be given enough power to carry out their assigned duties. At the same time, there also must be clear limits on the power they are given. Some questions you might use to consider the strengths and weaknesses of a position of authority include:

- Do people in the position have too many duties? Too few?

- Are people in the position given enough resources to fulfill their responsibilities?

- Are people in the position given enough power to do the job required? Are there clear limitations on this power?

- Are there adequate ways to hold persons accountable for fulfilling their responsibilities?

- Are there ways to prevent a misuse of power?

- Are there ways for people to express their opinions about how the duties are being performed?

- Are people in the position required to use fair procedures in fulfilling their responsibilities? Are they required to respect important values such as privacy, human dignity, and freedom?

Intellectual Tools Used to Examine Positions of Authority

The questions above form part of the intellectual tools you can use to evaluate a position of authority and determine if the position is well designed. Other questions you should answer are included in the intellectual tool chart on page 43. Study this chart carefully. You will have the opportunity to use it in the next lesson to evaluate a position of authority.

Using the Lesson

1. Write a short story in your journal about an imaginary country where there were no reasonable limitations on the powers of the president. Describe what might go wrong and what you would do to improve the situation.

2. Working with a study partner, select a position of authority to evaluate. Using the intellectual tools you have learned, identify the strengths and the weaknesses of the position. Consider whether you would recommend changes to improve the position. Give a speech to your class describing the position and explaining your views.

Intellectual Tool Chart for Evaluating Positions of Authority

Questions	Answers
1. What position of authority is to be evaluated?	
2. What is the purpose of the position?	
3. Is the position necessary? Why or why not?	
4. What are the duties, powers, privileges and limitations of the position?	
5. What might be the consequences of this position as it is designed?	
6. What are the weaknesses (if any) in the way the position is designed? Consider: ■ number of duties ■ resources provided ■ grant and limitation of power ■ accountability ■ controls to prevent misuse of authority ■ requirement of fair procedures and respect for important values	
7. What changes would you suggest to improve the position? What would be the benefits and costs of these changes?	
8. Do you think the position should be eliminated, left as it is, or changed? Explain your reasoning.	

LESSON 11

How Would You Improve This School Principal's Position?

Purpose of Lesson

In this lesson you will use the intellectual tools you have learned to evaluate how well a position of authority has been designed.

Critical Thinking Exercise
EVALUATING A POSITION OF AUTHORITY

Imagine that you are a member of the Midvale School District Board of Education. Recently, a problem has come up at Midvale High School which raises questions about the authority of a principal. It is your job to evaluate the position of school principal and suggest ways to improve it.

Work in small groups. Read the following selection, which includes a description of the principal's duties and powers, privileges, and limitations. Discuss the questions set forth in the Intellectual Tool Chart from Lesson 10 on page 43. Also discuss the questions which follow the selection. Select someone to note your answers. Be prepared to explain your suggestions about how the position could be improved.

Midvale High School

Midvale is a new school district. Until recently, Midvale had only a small elementary school. High school students had been bused almost thirty miles away. But last year a new high school was built in the town. With two schools, Midvale formed its own school district.

One of the first jobs of Midvale's Board of Education was to develop a job description for the position of high school principal. Last summer the board agreed on the following job description.

Duties and Powers. The principal has the duty and power to

- supervise all activities and operations of the school, including the purchase of necessary school equipment and the operation of the library and cafeteria

- assign teachers to the classes they will teach

- develop school rules regarding dress and behavior

- discipline students

Privileges. The principal is entitled to

- a salary higher than that paid to teachers

- a private office and a secretary

Limitations. The principal is required to

- have his or her performance reviewed once a year by the Board of Education

- keep school expenses within the budget

- obtain Board of Education approval before commenting on legal matters or issuing bulletins to the press or the community

- obey the limitations placed on all government officials by the Constitution

In March, a small group of students from Midvale High and their parents decided to express their opposition to the coal mines near Midvale. This group thought the mining companies were destroying the natural beauty of the area. As a protest, the students decided to wear black armbands to school to call attention to what they believed was the destruction of their environment.

The principal of Midvale High learned about the plan. He forbade students to wear black armbands to school. The protesting students were told the

rule. They knew they would be suspended if they wore the armbands.

For several days nothing happened. The principal was so busy trying to solve other problems, he couldn't get around to meeting with the parents of the protesting students. He wanted to publish a community bulletin explaining his rule against the armbands. That needed approval, however, and the Board of Education was not scheduled to meet for several weeks.

Then one day, seven students showed up for school wearing black armbands. There were no problems in the classes, but on the playground there were some angry remarks by children whose parents worked for the mining companies.

Later in the afternoon, the protesting students were called into the principal's office. They were told to remove the armbands. They refused. They were suspended until they returned to school without the armbands.

After suspending the students, the principal wrote a statement listing his reasons for forbidding the armbands. He said that Midvale families depended on the mining industry. Also, schools were no place for demonstrations. If a demonstration of this type occurred, it could interfere with classes and turn into something which would be very hard to control. The principal argued that it could lead to

- conflict between protesting students and students whose parents worked for the mining companies

- a long-term split between these two groups of students

- bad relations between people in the community

What do *you* think?

1. What problems or weaknesses do you see in the way the Midvale High School principal's job has been designed?

2. What changes would you suggest to improve this position of authority?

3. How would you evaluate the principal's decision to forbid the wearing of armbands to school? Do you agree or disagree with the arguments he used to justify this rule? Why?

Using the Lesson

1. Ask your librarian to help you research the United States Supreme Court's decision in the case of *Tinker v. Des Moines Independent Community School District*, 393 U.S. 503 (1969). Report what you learn to the class.

2. Suppose a person in a position of authority was not doing a good job. Describe things citizens could do to try to improve the situation. Make a poster or design a bulletin board to present your ideas.

LESSON 12

How Would You Evaluate the Supreme Court's Power of Judicial Review?

Purpose of Lesson

In this lesson you will use the intellectual tools you have studied to evaluate some of the powers and limitations of the Supreme Court, one of the most important institutions of our government. In particular, you will examine the Supreme Court's power of judical review. When you have completed this lesson, you should be able to explain and evaluate the Supreme Court's power of judicial review, and the limitations on that power.

Terms to Know

impeach
constitutional/unconstitutional
judicial review
ratify
equal protection of the laws
separate but equal doctrine
segregate
integrate

What does the Supreme Court do?

The Supreme Court of the United States is one of the most powerful institutions in our government. One of the most important duties of the Court is to decide disputes about the meaning of the Constitution and laws of the United States. Usually the Supreme Court reviews a case after it has first been decided by a lower court.

The Supreme Court does not have to consider and act upon every case brought to its attention. The Court chooses the cases it believes are most important to decide. Currently more than 4,000 cases per year are brought to the Supreme Court's attention, but the Court selects fewer than 200 cases per year to hear and decide. The cases it agrees to decide usually involve

- laws that might not be allowed by some part of the Constitution
- laws that may affect rights guaranteed to individuals by the Constitution

Supreme Court justices are appointed for life. This protects their independence. They can make decisions without having to worry if their decisions are unpopular. Even though Supreme Court justices are appointed for life, they may be **impeached**—charged and prosecuted—by Congress for misconduct in office. If found guilty, they are removed from office.

What is the power of judicial review?

One of the most important powers of the Court is to decide whether laws and actions of government agencies and officials are **unconstitutional**—in violation of the requirements of the Constitution —or **constitutional**—in accord with the requirements of the Constitution. In other words, the Court decides whether or not federal, state, and local laws, and actions of government are permitted by the Constitution. When the Supreme Court rules that a law is unconstitutional, the law may no longer be enforced. It is no longer a law.

The power to review laws and actions of government, and to decide whether they are constitutional, is called the power of **judicial review**. The power of judicial review is not mentioned specifically in the Constitution. However, the Constitution is "the supreme law of the land." Judicial review is based on the

Justices of the United States Supreme Court (1992–93)

argument that the Supreme Court must protect and enforce the Constitution. To do so, the Court must have the power to declare invalid any laws and actions of government that do not comply with the Constitution's requirements.

What are some limits on the power of judicial review?

As you know, the Constitution provides for the separation of powers and a system of "checks and balances" among the President, Congress and the Supreme Court—the executive, legislative, and judicial branches of the federal government. Even though the Supreme Court may exercise the power of judicial review to declare laws and actions of government unconstitutional, the Court's decision is not necessarily the last word on the subject. An amendment to the Constitution could be proposed by Congress which would have the effect of overriding the Court's decision. Before becoming effective, however, the amendment would have to be **ratified**, or

approved, by the state legislatures or by ratifying conventions in three-fourths of the states.

The Court's decisions also can be reversed by the Supreme Court itself. For example, in 1940 the Supreme Court upheld a law that required students to recite the Pledge of Allegiance. But that decision was overruled by the Court three years later, when the Court said that such laws violated the students' freedom of speech.

The Supreme Court does not have the physical power to enforce its decisions. For example, in the 1820s, the Court ruled that the Cherokee Indian Tribe had rights that the state of Georgia was required to respect. But President Andrew Jackson did nothing to enforce the Court's decision, and the Cherokees' rights were violated.

Nevertheless, the Supreme Court's decisions are regarded as law. Even the president of the United States is subject to the law of the land. In 1974, the Supreme Court ruled that President Richard Nixon was required to give certain tape recordings to a special prosecutor investigating the Watergate scandal. President Nixon obeyed the Court's decision, even though he had tried very hard to keep at least some of the tapes secret. Information on the tapes proved that President Nixon had known about and approved efforts to cover up crimes committed by people trying to help him win re-election. Disclosure of this information led to calls for President Nixon's impeachment and caused him to become the first U.S. president ever to resign from office.

Critical Thinking Exercise
EXAMINING POWERS AND LIMITATIONS OF THE SUPREME COURT

Work with a study partner to answer the following questions. Be prepared to discuss your answers with your class.

1. What is the purpose of the Supreme Court's power of judicial review?

2. Do you think the Supreme Court's power of judicial review is necessary? Why or why not?

3. What do you think are the advantages or benefits of appointing Supreme Court justices for life? What do you think are the disadvantages or costs? Do you think Supreme Court justices should be appointed for life? If not, what alternatives would you suggest? What would be the benefits and costs of these alternatives?

Critical Thinking Exercise
ANALYZING AND EVALUATING THE POWER OF JUDICIAL REVIEW

The following is a brief summary of the facts and effects of one of the most famous cases decided by the Supreme Court. This is the case of *Brown v. Board of Education* (1954). As you read this selection, try to determine what changes, if any, you would make in the Court's power of judicial review. Then work in small groups to answer the questions which follow the selection. Be prepared to share your answers with your class.

Brown v. Board of Education

In 1954, the United States Supreme Court decided a case which has had far-reaching effects in this country. It involved an eight-year-old child, Linda Brown, who lived in Topeka, Kansas. Linda could not attend a public elementary school that was five blocks from her home. Only white children were permitted to attend that school. Linda had to go to school twenty-one blocks away, because the law in Topeka required African-American children and white children to attend separate schools.

Linda's parents, Mr. and Mrs. George Brown, believed the law was unfair. They decided to challenge it. Instead of sending Linda to the school for black children, they took her to the school for white children. They asked that she be enrolled there. When the school authorities refused, the Browns went to court. Eventually, the United States Supreme Court agreed to hear the case.

The Browns were represented by Thurgood Marshall, who later became a justice of the Supreme Court, and other lawyers from the National Association for the Advancement of Colored People (NAACP). They argued that having separate schools for blacks and whites was unconstitutional. They said this policy violated the Constitution's requirement that government

NAACP lawyers George Hayes, Thurgood Marshall, and James Nabrit (1954)

How are the decisions of the Supreme Court enforced?

must not discriminate unfairly against people—that all people must receive **equal protection of the laws.**

Lawyers for the Topeka Board of Education argued that schools in Topeka were equal in terms of buildings, courses of study, and quality of teachers. They pointed to earlier cases the Supreme Court had decided. In these cases the Court had upheld laws which required separate facilities for blacks and whites. The Court's decisions had been based on the argument that the facilities for blacks were equal to the facilities for whites. The rule of these earlier decisions was known as the **"separate but equal" doctrine.**

But in 1954 the Supreme Court ruled in favor of the Browns. The Court said that the "separate but equal" doctrine could not justify **segregated** (racially separate) schools. Linda Brown and other children in her situation had not received the equal protection of the laws guaranteed by the Constitution. Public schools would have to be **integrated**—students of all races must be permitted to attend.

The decision required that schools be integrated as quickly as possible. But many people opposed the decision. In 1957 the governor of Arkansas refused to comply with orders to integrate the schools. President Dwight Eisenhower sent soldiers to Little Rock, Arkansas to enforce the Court's decision. They escorted black children to and from school.

Ten years later most schools were still segregated. But people were encouraged by other Supreme Court decisions which overruled the "separate but equal" doctrine and prohibited government from operating segregated swimming pools, golf courses, and other public facilities. Many people joined together in the Civil Rights Movement and protested the treatment of blacks as second-class citizens. Led by Martin Luther King, Jr., hundreds of thousands of people assembled in Washington, D.C. and demonstrated against racial discrimination. The Civil Rights Movement persuaded Congress to pass laws in 1964 making discrimination illegal. While racial discrimination is still a serious problem in the United States, legally enforced segregation is a thing of the past.

How did the actions of Martin Luther King, Jr., and other private citizens help end segregation?

What do *you* think?

1. What issue did the Supreme Court have to decide in *Brown vs. Board of Education*? What decision did the Court make in this case?

2. What were some effects of the Supreme Court's decision in this case? In what ways was the Court's decision not effective?

3. Keeping in mind your answers to the previous questions, what strengths and weaknesses do you see in the way the Supreme Court's power of judicial review is designed?

4. What changes, if any, would you make in the Supreme Court's power of judicial review and in the limitations on that power? What would be the benefits and costs of these changes? Explain your position.

Using the Lesson

1. The Supreme Court has been given the power to declare a law passed by a majority of a legislature to be unconstitutional. What arguments can you give for and against giving the Court such power? Make a chart to present your arguments. You and some classmates might also like to present a debate on this issue.

2. Review newspapers and magazines to identify one case currently being reviewed by the Supreme Court. What rights and interests are involved in the case? What might be the effects if the Court rules that the laws or actions in the case are unconstitutional? Do these possible effects suggest the Supreme Court has too much power? Not enough? Why?

Lesson 13

How Would You Create a Position of Authority?

Purpose of Lesson

In this lesson you will use what you have learned to design a position of authority. This position of authority will deal with environmental problems in the imaginary city of Rivertown. When you have completed this lesson, you should be able to design the duties, powers, privileges, and limitations of a position of authority.

Critical Thinking Exercise
DESIGNING A POSITION OF AUTHORITY

In this exercise you will act as a member of the Rivertown City Council and create a position of authority. To begin, read the story, "Cleaning Up the Environment." Then break into small groups and follow the instructions.

Cleaning Up the Environment

Rivertown is small, but it shares the problems of most American cities. One concern is to protect the environment and improve the quality of life for the people in Rivertown. During much of the past year, the city council has been investigating a number of environmental issues.

Council members have been particularly worried about the contamination of Lake Minona. The lake lies on the southern border of the town. It supplies both fresh water and fish to local residents. Because of inadequate sewage treatment facilities, untreated sewage from the city runs off into Lake Minona. This raw sewage has forced authorities to close the beach on a number of occasions.

There is an even more serious problem, however—chemical pollution. In recent years,

How would you design a position of authority to deal with environmental problems?

What arguments can you make to support the position of authority you have designed?

local factories, including Rivertown's largest industry, have allowed harmful chemicals to flow into the lake water. Last spring the state department of health advised that no local fish should be eaten until the lake water was purified.

The city council held a series of public hearings. Testimony was given by a number of experts, including two professors from the state university. Members of the state department of health, local doctors, and hospital personnel spoke of the potential health hazards from the lake. On the other hand, representatives of the Chamber of Commerce, trade unions, and local business and industry spoke of the costs that would be involved in cleaning up the lake and in preventing future pollution. They argued that these costs could force factories to close and make people lose their jobs.

A number of proposals were made to clean up Lake Minona. Members of the city council are torn. They agree about the need to clean up the lake and prevent future industrial pollution. At the same time, they are aware of the costs involved and the risk to local industry. They are concerned that some companies may leave Rivertown rather than comply with more burdensome environmental controls.

Pollution of Lake Minona is the most serious environmental concern before the city council, but it is not the only one. Other proposals have been made about controlling air pollution and recycling garbage. Council members feel they need to create a position of authority in city government to deal with environmental matters. But what kind of position?

- Should there be one person in charge of environmental issues or two, one responsible for residential problems and one for industrial? Or should a committee be in charge of environmental issues instead of one or two people?

- Should the new position be elected or appointed?

- What duties, powers, privileges, and limitations should the position of authority have?

The Rivertown City Council decided to set up a committee to investigate the alternatives and come up with a plan of action.

Directions for the Committees

Each group is responsible for developing a new position of authority to deal with the environmental problems in Rivertown. Select a chairperson to help lead your discussion and someone to take notes.

On page 54 you will find the Intellectual Tool Chart for Designing Positions of Authority. The questions on the chart should be considered when designing your position of authority. Be sure your group reads, discusses, and answers each question carefully.

Presenting Your Plan

1. Each group should prepare a presentation describing its proposed position of authority. The presentation should include the following sections:

   ■ a statement of the purpose of the position

   ■ a list of its duties, powers, privileges, and limitations

   ■ a list of the probable effects (the costs and benefits) of the position as it has been planned

2. Each group will have three minutes to present its plan. Questions may be asked of group members.

3. After all presentations have been completed, the class should discuss the strengths and weaknesses of each proposed position. Individuals may offer changes in any plan.

4. A vote should then be held on which position of authority seems best designed to deal with the environmental issues confronting the Rivertown City Council.

Using the Lesson

1. Do you personally agree with the decision of your class about how to deal with the environmental problems in Rivertown? Write a letter to the editor of the Rivertown newspaper supporting or opposing the proposed new position of authority, or draw a cartoon to illustrate your views.

2. Think about an environmental problem in your neighborhood or town that might be helped by creating a position of authority. Use what you have learned in this unit to design a position of authority to deal with this problem. You may wish to create a photo collage to illustrate your ideas.

3. Choose a position of authority in your school, state, or nation that you think needs to be redesigned. Draw a chart or write a short essay showing how you would improve this position.

Intellectual Tool Chart for Designing Positions of Authority

Questions	Answers
1. What problem or problems are you trying to solve?	
2. Would establishing a position of authority help, or are there better ways to deal with the problem? Explain your views.	
3. What type of position of authority is your group suggesting: ■ one position or more than one? ■ individual or committee? ■ elected or appointed? Explain the reasons for your choices.	
4. What duties, powers, privileges, and limitations should the position of authority have? Consider: ■ number of duties ■ resources provided ■ grant and limitation of power ■ accountability ■ controls to prevent misuse of authority ■ requirement of fair procedures and respect for important values	
5. What would be the probable effects of having such a position of authority? Consider the benefits and costs of the position as you have designed it.	

PRIVACY
Table of Contents

Introduction

Supreme Court Justice Louis D. Brandeis (1856–1941), an early champion of the right to privacy.

"The right of the people to be secure in their persons, houses, papers, and effects, against unreasonable searches and seizures, shall not be violated ...."

The Fourth Amendment to the United States Constitution, quoted above, requires the government to respect our right to privacy. The right to privacy is one of the most important protections of human freedom and dignity we have. Privacy is valuable not only for itself, but also for the enjoyment of our rights to property and to freedom of thought, expression, religion, and conscience. Without the right to privacy, these other important rights would not mean very much at all.

But the right to privacy is not absolute. There are times when an individual's right to privacy must be limited to protect society's need for order and for information. As Americans, we need to be able to think and decide for ourselves when it is reasonable to limit our right to privacy in order to protect other important interests of our society.

This study of privacy should help you gain a greater understanding of its importance. It should also help you deal more effectively with issues of privacy as they arise in your daily life as an individual in a free society.

Unit One: What Is the Importance of Privacy?

Why is privacy important?

Purpose of Unit

This unit will help you develop a greater understanding of the meaning of privacy. You will learn to identify and describe examples of privacy in a variety of situations and to discriminate between situations in which privacy does and does not exist.

You also will learn some common ways people behave to protect their privacy, and you will examine the privacy needs of organizations and institutions.

Lesson 1

What Is Privacy?

Purpose of Lesson

This lesson defines privacy as it is used in this textbook. When you have completed this lesson, you should be able to distinguish between situations in which privacy does and does not exist. You also should be able to describe common objects of privacy and the reasons why people may wish to have privacy in specific situations.

Terms to Know

privacy
object of privacy
solitude

What is privacy?

Privacy involves the "right to be left alone." This right can be threatened or invaded in different

Why do people need privacy?

ways. People say "leave me alone" when someone asks them questions they do not want to answer. People also say "leave me alone" when they want someone to go away, and when someone is bothering them, or interfering with something they are trying to do. Thus, the right to privacy may include:

- the right to decide whether information will be shared with others

- the right to **solitude**—the state of being alone, away from other people

- the right to be free from the interference of others

The things we want to keep others from finding out about, observing, or interfering with are called **"objects of privacy."** Objects of privacy may include:

- **facts** such as where you were born, who your parents are, what your age or weight is

- **actions** such as where you go or who you see

- **places and possessions** such as your room or the contents of a box or closet

- **thoughts and feelings** such as who you like and dislike, what you are afraid of, what your religious or political beliefs are

- **communications** such as your letters or telephone conversations

Critical Thinking Exercise
IDENTIFYING AND EXAMINING SITUATIONS INVOLVING PRIVACY

Read the following situations. List the numbers of the situations which are examples of privacy. Next write your answers to the questions that follow. Be prepared to share your answers with your class.

1. Alex went into his room to talk on the telephone with his girlfriend because he didn't want his sister, Laura, to hear him.

2. Sometimes Valerie went up on the roof to be alone when she practiced her guitar so people wouldn't hear her trying to learn to play.

3. Tony walked up to Marsha and said, "The baseball season starts today."

4. Coretta and Maria were best friends. They had a place in the mall where they met on Saturdays, but they agreed not to let anyone else know where it was.

5. Tom and Becky were looking around in an old cave when suddenly some rocks came tumbling down and closed off the mouth of the cave. Tom and Becky yelled for help, but no one could hear them. Now they were really alone.

6. When Larry received a D in mathematics on his report card, he kept it secret from his friends.

7. Although Carlos supported the Republican candidate for president, he didn't speak about it at work, because his boss supported the Democratic candidate.

Examining the Situations

Answer the following questions for each situation that is an example of privacy.

1. **Why** is this situation an example of privacy?

2. **Who** wants to keep something private?

3. What is the **object of privacy**?

4. From **whom** is something to be kept private?

5. **Why** do you suppose the person wanted privacy?

Using the Lesson

1. Write several rules that you would like to see people obey to protect your privacy at school. Be prepared to explain your rules to your class.

2. Bring a news clipping to class or report on a TV news program which illustrates an issue involving privacy. Be prepared to explain the issue to your classmates.

3. While you are studying privacy, keep a privacy notebook or journal. For the next twenty-four hours, identify at least five situations involving privacy. Write entries in your journal explaining the situations, stating who wishes to keep something private, what the object of privacy is, and from whom the person wants to keep the object private. Then explain why the person might have wanted to keep the object private.

Lesson 2

How Do People Maintain Their Privacy?

Purpose of Lesson

This lesson describes different ways people behave to maintain their privacy. When you have finished this lesson, you should be able to explain some common ways people behave to keep others from observing or finding out about objects of privacy.

Terms to Know

isolation
secrecy
confidentiality
exclusion

How do people behave to keep things private?

The following are some of the most common ways that people behave to protect their privacy.

1. **Isolation**. People may **isolate** themselves, that is, they may keep away from other people. For example, they may stay in a room or a house or go to some far-away place to live.

2. **Secrecy**. People may keep objects of privacy **secret**, that is, they may purposely not tell others about them. For example, you and your friends may keep your plans for a weekend a secret, or agree not to tell anyone about something you have seen or done. People may keep facts about their income or their debts a secret.

3. **Confidentiality**. When private information is shared with someone who is expected and trusted not to tell anyone else, this is called **confidentiality**. For example, you may tell a secret to a friend, a relative, or a guidance counselor, and expect the information not to be repeated. What people say in private to their doctors, lawyers, and religious counselors is confidential.

4. **Exclusion**. People may keep things private or secret by **excluding** others. For example, you may keep something private by not allowing others to look into your wallet, your locker, your room, or your home. Some government agencies try to maintain secrecy by not allowing unauthorized people to go into certain buildings or on the grounds of military bases.

Critical Thinking Exercise
IDENTIFYING THE MEANS USED TO MAINTAIN PRIVACY

As you read the following excerpt adapted from *The Adventures of Tom Sawyer* by Mark Twain, try to identify the different ways people behave to keep things private. Then answer the questions that follow. Be prepared to discuss your answers with the class.

Excerpt from *The Adventures of Tom Sawyer*

Tom Sawyer and Huckleberry Finn are at the graveyard one night when Dr. Robinson shows up with Muff Potter and a man named Joe to rob the grave of Hoss Williams. As the men approach, Tom and Huck hide behind a tree to avoid being seen. After they have dug up Hoss Williams' body, Muff Potter and Joe demand more money than the agreed amount Dr. Robinson had already paid them. As Joe explains to Dr. Robinson, he has an old score to settle:

"Five years ago you drove me away from your father's kitchen one night, when I come to ask for

something to eat, and you said I warn't there for any good; and when I swore I'd get even with you if it took a hundred years, your father had me jailed for a vagrant. Did you think I'd forget? And now I've *got* you, and you got to *settle*, you know!"

He was threatening the doctor, with his fist in his face, by this time. The doctor struck out suddenly and stretched the ruffian on the ground. Potter dropped his knife, and exclaimed:

"Here, now, don't you hit my pard!" and the next moment he had grappled with the doctor and the two were struggling with might and main, trampling the grass and tearing the ground with their heels. Joe sprang to his feet, his eyes flaming with passion, snatched up Potter's knife, and went creeping, catlike and stooping, round and round about the combatants, seeking an opportunity. All at once the doctor flung himself free, seized the heavy headboard of Williams' grave and felled Potter to the earth with it—and in the same instant Joe saw his chance and drove the knife to the hilt in the young man's breast. He reeled and fell partly on Potter, flooding him with his blood, and in the same moment the clouds blotted out the dreadful spectacle and the two frightened boys went speeding away in the dark.

After Muff Potter comes to, Joe tricks him into thinking that he, rather than Joe, has killed the doctor.

The two boys flew on and on, toward the village, speechless with horror. They glanced backward over their shoulders from time to time, apprehensively, as if they feared they might be followed. Every stump that started up in their path seemed a man and an enemy, and made them catch their breath; and as they sped by some outlying cottages that lay near the village, the barking of the aroused watch-dogs seemed to give wings to their feet.

"If we can only get to the old tannery before we break down!" whispered Tom, in short catches between breaths, "I can't stand it much longer."

Huckleberry's hard pantings were his only reply, and the boys fixed their eyes on the goal of their hopes and bent to their work to win it. They gained steadily on it, and at last, breast to breast, they burst through the open door and fell grateful and exhausted in the sheltering shadows beyond. By and by their pulses slowed down, and Tom whispered:

"Huckleberry, what do you reckon'll come of this?"

"If Dr. Robinson dies, I reckon a hanging'll come of it."

Tom thought awhile, then he said:

"Who'll tell? We?"

"What are you talking about? S'pose something happened and Joe *didn't* hang? Why he'd kill us some time or other, just as dead sure as we're a-laying here."

"That's just what I was thinking to myself, Huck."

"If anybody tells, let Muff Potter do it, if he's fool enough. He's generally drunk enough."

Tom said nothing—went on thinking. Presently he whispered:

"Huck, Muff Potter don't *know* it. How can he tell?

"What's the reason he don't know it?"

"Because he just got that whack when Joe done it. D'you reckon he could see anything? D'you reckon he knowed anything?"

"By hokey, that's so, Tom!"

After another reflective silence, Tom said:

"Hucky, you sure you can keep mum?"

"Tom, we *got* to keep mum. *You* know that. That devil wouldn't make any more of drownding us than a couple of cats, if we was to squeak 'bout this and they didn't hang him. Now, look-a-here, Tom, less take and swear to one another—that's what we got to do—swear to keep mum."

"I'm agreed. It's the best thing. Would you just hold hands and swear that we—"

"Oh, no, that wouldn't do for this. That's good enough for little rubbishy common things—but there orter be writing 'bout a big thing like this. And blood."

Tom's whole being applauded this idea. It was deep, and dark, and awful; the hour, the circumstances, the surroundings, were in keeping with it. He picked up a clean pine shingle that lay in the moonlight, took a little fragment of "red keel" out of his pocket, got the moon on his work, and painfully scrawled these lines, emphasizing each slow down-stroke by clamping his tongue between his teeth, and letting up the pressure on the up-strokes:

> "Huck Finn and Tom Sawyer Swears they will keep mum about this and they wish they may drop down dead in their tracks if they ever tell and Rot."

"Huck Finn and Tom Sawyer swears they will keep mum about this and they wish they may Drop down dead in their tracks if they ever tell and Rot."

Huckleberry was filled with admiration of Tom's facility in writing, and the sublimity of his language. Tom unwound the thread from one of his needles, and each boy pricked the ball of his thumb and squeezed out a drop of blood. In time, after many squeezes, Tom managed to sign his initials, using the ball of his little finger for a pen. Then he showed Huckleberry how to make an H and an F, and the oath was complete. They buried the shingle close to the wall, with some dismal ceremonies and incantations, and the fetters that bound their tongues were considered to be locked and the key thrown away.

"Tom," whispered Huckleberry, "does this keep us from *ever* telling—*always?*"

"Of course it does. It don't make any difference *what* happens, we got to keep mum. We'd drop down dead—don't *you* know that?"

"Yes, I reckon that's so."

Identifying Different Means of Maintaining Privacy

1. Who in the story wished to keep something private or secret?

2. What did they wish to keep secret?

3. From whom did they wish to keep something secret?

4. How did they behave in order to maintain privacy or keep secrets?

5. What examples in the story are there of a) isolation, b) secrecy, c) confidentiality, and d) exclusion?

Using the Lesson

1. Draw a picture or make a collage to illustrate each of the four means people use to maintain privacy that are described in this lesson (isolation, secrecy, confidentiality, and exclusion).

2. Why might it be important to protect confidential communications, such as those with a doctor or lawyer, from being disclosed? Are there any circumstances when such confidential communications should be disclosed? Explain your answer.

3. Later in *The Adventures of Tom Sawyer*, Muff Potter is arrested and put on trial for the murder of Dr. Robinson. Tom has to decide if he should violate his oath to Huck Finn and testify about what really happened, or keep silent and let an innocent man hang. If you were Tom Sawyer, what would you do? Why?

Lesson 3

Why Might Institutions Need to Maintain Secrecy?

Purpose of Lesson

This lesson introduces the subject of institutional secrecy. When you have finished this lesson, you should be able to explain why various private and public organizations or institutions may wish to keep things secret.

Term to Know

institution

What is an institution?

Institutions are established organizations, such as

- schools and universities
- business corporations
- museums
- hospitals
- federal, state, and local governments

Like individuals, institutions try to keep certain things private. For example, hospitals want to keep medical records private. Schools and universities want to keep student records private. Museums may want to keep their plans for buying new works of art private. Business corporations usually want to keep plans for new products and plans for distributing and advertising them secret. Many governments have secret weapons or secret military plans; they may have spies whose names are secret, and they often have letters and other documents that they want to keep secret.

Critical Thinking Exercise
EXAMINING INSTITUTIONAL SECRECY

As you read the following story, try to find out what the school wanted to keep secret and why.

Then answer the questions that follow. Be prepared to discuss your answers with your class.

The Nomination Committee

Ricardo Ruiz was a member of the nomination committee and he was angry as he waited outside the principal's office. He had to talk with Ms. Hunter about a problem. It was a problem that could ruin his whole plan.

The plan he and his friends had thought up was that this year a committee of ninth graders at Palmer High School, instead of teachers or the principal, would choose the "outstanding graduate."

It was important to Ricardo to make this plan work. He felt that too often the teachers looked only at a student's grades and overlooked other things that were important. Ricardo had nominated Kevin Taylor. Kevin had good grades, but not as good as many other students. But Kevin had prevented a fight between two students who were members of rival gangs at the school, and he had helped to set up a tutoring program.

When all the nominations had been made, the student committee asked the principal for copies of the school records of the six nominees. The committee wanted to be sure they had any information which might help them make the decision.

That was why Ricardo Ruiz was sitting outside Ms. Hunter's office. She had refused to give the committee the school's files on the six nominees. And that made him angry.

Ms. Hunter came to the door and asked Ricardo to come in and sit down.

"I know why you're here," she said. "And I hope I can explain why it has to be this way."

Why might schools need to keep certain records private?

"You don't have to explain," Ricardo answered. "We know the school doesn't want the student committee to make this decision. You think we will make a wrong choice. So you decided not to let us have the information we needed."

"That's not true Ricardo," Ms. Hunter replied. "We want you to make the choice. And we know the information in these files might help. But the school has a responsibility to keep these files secret. They can only be used for certain reasons. It wouldn't be right to let everyone look at students' records. Would you like everybody to look at your records?"

"No, I guess not," Ricardo shrugged. "But each of the nominees said it would be all right if the committee saw their files. Shouldn't that make it OK?"

"There are other people we have to consider also," said Ms. Hunter. "The school has a responsibility to the teachers who have written things on those records. Teachers don't expect students to see those records. And parents expect that notes they write to the school will be kept confidential. They have a right to privacy, too. It was a tough decision for us to make. You know, Ricardo, individuals aren't the only ones with secrets. Sometimes, schools have secrets, too."

Examining Secrecy

1. What things does the school want to keep secret?

2. From whom does the school wish to keep the information secret?

3. How does the school plan to keep the information secret?

4. Why does the school want to keep the information secret?

5. How might Ricardo and the committee try to convince the school to show them the candidates' school records, or give them the information they need from the records?

6. How do you think this conflict over the privacy of the school records should be resolved?

Using the Lesson

1. What other institutions might have information about people that they want to keep secret? What kind of information might they want to keep secret? Why? Draw a picture to illustrate your answers.

2. What information might you want that an institution could refuse to give to you because it is secret? Should it be kept secret? Why?

3. Do you think there are some kinds of information which our government should be allowed to keep secret? What are some different reasons the government might want to keep a secret? Do you think there are some kinds of information which the government should **not** be allowed to keep secret, even if it wants to? Explain your position.

4. Do research to learn about the "Pentagon Papers" lawsuit [*New York Times Co. v. United States* 403 U.S. 713 (1971)], or about another time someone challenged a government agency's effort to keep a secret. Then prepare a brief report describing what happened. State what you learned concerning the circumstances in which the government should and should not be allowed to keep secrets from its citizens.

Unit Two: What Factors Explain Differences in Privacy Behavior?

How do city dwellers create opportunities for privacy?

Purpose of Unit

This unit will introduce you to the factors or elements that explain differences in the privacy behavior of individuals. You will learn that although privacy exists in all cultures, there are often differences in the privacy behavior of individuals within a culture and between different cultures. You will examine some areas in which differences are common and examine the reasons for the differences you identify.

Lesson 4

Why Might People's Privacy Behavior Differ?

Purpose of Lesson

This lesson examines some of the common reasons for the differences in privacy behavior among people. When you have finished this lesson, you should be able to describe and explain similarities and differences in privacy behavior.

Terms to Know

factor
occupation
role
values

What factors influence privacy behavior?

People may differ in the objects they wish to keep private and in ways they behave to keep these objects secret. What can explain these differences? Various **factors**, or elements, in people's lives explain differences in their privacy behavior. The following are some factors that typically influence a person's privacy behavior.

1. **Family.** A person's family environment may influence his or her privacy behavior. For example:

   ▪ In Nancy's family, no one ever mentions Uncle Jack because he has had several brushes with the law and served time in prison.

   ▪ Betty, her parents, and her six brothers and sisters all live together in a two-bedroom apartment. Betty loves to draw. But sometimes she has a difficult time working on her art projects because other members of her family are always

around. So she often goes to the park and draws. She dreams of a time when she can have her own room where she can be alone to draw.

How can family environment influence a person's privacy behavior?

2. **Occupation or role.** A person's job or role may require the person to maintain privacy. For example:

   ▪ Mickey had been a child TV star ever since he played Little Louie in the long-running series, "Dewey Goes to College." As he has grown older, it has become more and more difficult for Mickey to play the parts of young people. And that is why Mickey doesn't want anyone to know his real age. He wants people to believe that he's younger than he really is.

   ▪ Sarah works on top secret projects for the Department of Defense. She is sworn to secrecy and cannot even discuss her work with her son or her closest friend.

How can individual experiences influence a person's privacy behavior?

3. **Individual experiences**. Past experiences may influence how a person wants to live in order to maintain privacy. For example:

   ■ Martin was really embarrassed once when a friend he trusted revealed to the entire class that Martin had a crush on Leslie. Now, though many years have passed, Martin doesn't often share his feelings, even with his friends.

   ■ In Maria's family most problems were discussed openly. When she became an adult, there were very few things she would not discuss with her friends.

4. **Opportunities for privacy.** People's behavior may be influenced by the opportunities for privacy that exist in their environment. For example:

   ■ Judy grew up on a small farm. The nearest neighbor lived more than a mile away, and it took half an hour to drive to the nearest town. She liked living there and being alone with her family. In her spare time Judy worked on her computer. She became quite an expert. When she heard about job opportunities in Chicago, she decided to move to the big city. Judy was hired by a large company, and did

her job very well. She was promoted several times, took on more and more responsibility, and was paid very well for her work. But Judy never got used to the crowds and noise of the city. After a lot of thought, she decided to quit her job and move back to her parents' farm, where she and her family could live undisturbed.

   ■ In his book *1984*, George Orwell described a society in which there was a special television screen ("telescreen") in every home. This telescreen allowed the government to watch and listen to everything people did. The main character, Winston Smith, found a tiny room above a shop that did not have a telescreen. Even though it was small and run-down, it was like paradise for Winston.

5. **Value placed on privacy.** People's behavior may differ depending on the value they, their family, or their culture place on privacy. For example:

   ■ In medieval Europe people "went to the bathroom" by the side of the road, and did not care if they were seen by others.

- In some Muslim countries women wear veils over their faces and robes which fully cover their bodies to protect their privacy.

6. **Competing values.** Although people may value privacy highly, sometimes other things may be more important to them in specific situations. For example:

   - In *The Adventures of Tom Sawyer*, Tom Sawyer considers whether he should testify at the murder trial of Muff Potter, even though he has promised Huck Finn he would never tell anyone what they had seen. Tom wants to keep the information secret, but he decides it is more important to save Muff Potter from a hanging he doesn't deserve.

7. **Individual differences** sometimes lead people to make **different choices** with regard to privacy. For example:

   - Randy and Sharon are students at Rivercrest Junior High. They each have many friends and enjoy talking with them. When Randy talks to his friends, he tells them just about everything. But Sharon keeps some things to herself.

   Once somebody overheard Randy talking with his best friend. Sharon asked Randy if this bothered him. Randy replied, "Not really. It's important to me to be able to talk to my good friends. If somebody overhears what I say, it's no big deal. I've got nothing to hide."

Critical Thinking Exercise
EXAMINING PRIVACY BEHAVIOR

Work with a study partner to answer the following questions. You may use the examples of privacy behavior you have just read, or examples from your own experience or imagination, to explain your answers. Be prepared to discuss your answers with the class.

1. How might a person's family environment and past experiences influence his or her privacy behavior?

2. How might a person's occupation or role require him or her to maintain privacy?

3. How might differences in people's values explain differences in their privacy behavior?

4. How might differences in the opportunities for privacy explain differences in privacy behavior?

Using the Lesson

1. How does your privacy behavior compare with the privacy behavior described in the examples in this lesson? What factors explain the similarities and differences?

2. What factors explain the differences between your privacy behavior and that of your friends? What factors explain the similarities?

3. Should people in certain jobs (top athletes or public officials, for example) be allowed less privacy than the rest of us? Why or why not?

4. Describe how the occupations of the following people might influence their own needs for privacy:

magician	movie actor
inventor	politician
writer	lawyer

5. Explain why the occupations of the following people might lead them to invade the privacy of others:

newspaper reporter	talk-show host
police officer	doctor
private investigator	psychiatrist

   How might these occupations also require people to protect the privacy of others?

Lesson 5

How Do Different Cultures Deal with Privacy?

Purpose of Lesson

This lesson provides an opportunity to examine some ways that different cultures deal with privacy. When you have finished the lesson, you should be able to explain cultural similarities and differences in privacy behavior.

Term to Know

culture

Differences Among Cultures

The term **"culture"** is used in various senses, but in this text we use the term to refer to a people's whole way of life. Culture includes customs, habits, family structure, political life, religion, economic and legal systems, arts, science, educational institutions and ideals. Culture is a way of life that lasts over time and is passed on from one generation to another.

Privacy is found in all cultures. People of various cultures, however, may differ in the **objects they choose to keep private** and the **means they use to maintain privacy**. For example, some people think their age should be kept private. Others may reveal their age, yet think their religious or political beliefs should be private. In some cultures, people always eat in private; it is considered indecent to eat in public.

People also may differ in the ways they maintain privacy. For example, in some cultures homes are built with soundproof walls to promote privacy. In other cultures, walls may be thin and sound can easily be heard through them. In such cultures, people maintain a sense of privacy by purposely not listening or by pretending not to overhear one another.

Cultures are complicated. In some cases, people of one culture might be uncomfortable if they are more than one foot away from others while talking to them. On the other hand, people from another culture might be uncomfortable if others get as close as one foot to them. Can you imagine what happens when people from these different cultures try to talk to each other!

In the exercises below, you will have the opportunity to examine the privacy behavior of people with cultures different from our own.

Critical Thinking Exercise
EXAMINING PRIVACY BEHAVIOR

Read the following selection carefully. As you do, identify the privacy behavior of the Mehinacu people. Think about what might explain their behavior and be prepared to discuss your answers to the questions that follow.

How could you maintain a sense of privacy in a house with paper-thin walls?

The Mehinacu People

The Mehinacu are a people who live in central Brazil. Their houses are made from the leaves of trees. The houses are built around a central square or plaza. The paths to the farming fields, the harbor, and the bathing area are wide and open. This allows anyone who is using these roads to be easily seen by other people. It is no trouble for a Mehinacu to hear conversations through the thin walls of the houses. Everybody knows everyone else's business.

How do the Mehinacu get any privacy? They try in many different ways. One rule of the Mehinacu culture says that Mehinacu women are not allowed to enter the Men's House. The Men's House is a small building which the men use on both religious and social occasions.

Another rule says that a Mehinacu cannot go into any house that is not his or her own. This means that conversations often take place through the walls of the houses. Within the house, there are areas which are off-limits to certain family members. If there is a change in a person's social status (for example, if a person is preparing to become a chief), barriers are set up around that person. He or she can then be all alone for a certain period of time.

There are other ways that the Mehinacu try to get privacy. Hidden paths and secret bathing areas exist so that people can have privacy if they want it. According to custom, a person should not tell others when another person is doing something wrong or illegal. People pretend to be unaware of things which are happening right in front of them.

A Privacy Chart for the Mehinacu People		
What are the objects of privacy?	From whom are they to be kept private?	How are they to be kept private?

What do *you* think?

1. What are some of the similarities and differences in the privacy behavior of the Mehinacu people compared with yours?

2. What explanations can you give for these similarities and differences?

3. Have you ever met someone from a different culture? What differences did you notice in their privacy behavior?

4. Why do you think people of all cultures need some form of privacy?

Critical Thinking Exercise
EXAMINING PRIVACY BEHAVIOR

As you read the following selection, think about how you might feel if you lived in the imaginary society it describes. What would your privacy behavior be like? What factors would explain your privacy behavior?

1984 is a novel by George Orwell. It describes a society in which human thought and action are controlled by the Ruling Party. On many buildings, the Party has put up huge posters showing the face of a man. The pictures are made so that the eyes seem to follow you when you move. Under each picture are the words: BIG BROTHER IS WATCHING YOU.

Inside every person's apartment is a special television screen (or "telescreen"). There is no way to turn it off. The telescreen shows programs just as an ordinary television set does, but it also does much more. It picks up any sounds made in the apartment. As long as people stay within the field of vision of the telescreen, they can be seen and heard by the Thought Police. Any action or conversation in the house can be observed. Any object taken into the home can be discovered through the telescreen.

How would you feel if everything you did could be seen and heard?

There is no way for people to know whether or not they are being watched at any given moment. The Thought Police may be watching them all the time. Maybe they are only being watched some of the time. No one knows for sure. But one thing is certain: the Thought Police can watch them any time they want to. People have to live with the possibility that every sound they make is overhead and that (except when there is total darkness) every movement is watched.

What do *you* think?

1. What might people in this imaginary society want to keep private?

2. How might they try to keep it private?

3. What are some factors which might affect the privacy behavior of people in this imaginary society?

Using the Lesson

1. As you watch a television program, think about the privacy behavior of the main character. What does that character want to keep private? How does he or she go about getting privacy? What do you think could explain the character's privacy behavior? Write your answers to these questions and discuss them in class.

2. Write a story about a person living in the United States who wants to keep something private. In your story, describe what the person wants to keep private. Be sure to include what you think are the reasons for the person's privacy behavior.

3. In your privacy notebook or journal, write at least three or four questions you have about privacy. The questions might be about the reasons or the ways people seek privacy, the similarities or the differences in the privacy behavior of different people, or the impact of privacy on people or on society, for example.

Unit Three: What Are Some Benefits and Costs of Privacy?

What might be some of the benefits and costs of a doctor or lawyer respecting the privacy of a client?

Purpose of Unit

Every time we maintain privacy there are certain consequences. Some consequences are **benefits,** or advantages; some are **costs,** or disadvantages. Knowing the consequences of privacy can help us make decisions about issues of privacy. For example, if you are trying to decide in a particular situation whether a claim to privacy should be recognized, you need to think about what the benefits and costs might be of maintaining privacy in the situation.

In this unit, you will learn to identify some common benefits and costs of privacy. You also will learn that different individuals may have different opinions about whether the right to privacy should be protected in a particular situation.

Lesson 6

What Are the Possible Consequences of Privacy?

Purpose of Lesson

This lesson examines some of the possible consequences of privacy. You will classify these consequences as benefits or costs. Later, you will be asked to evaluate positions on issues of privacy by thinking about the consequences of privacy. When you have completed this lesson you should be able to explain some common benefits and costs of privacy.

Terms to Know

benefits	Writs of Assistance
costs	conformity
totalitarian	creativity
intellectual stimulation	

Critical Thinking Exercise
IDENTIFYING CONSEQUENCES OF PRIVACY

Your class should be divided into small groups. Each group should read the situations below and list the possible consequences of privacy in each situation. Next, the group should classify these consequences as **benefits** (advantages) or as **costs** (disadvantages). Each group then should share its lists of benefits and costs with the class.

1. Before the American Revolution, English officials in the colonies were able to use general search warrants, called **Writs of Assistance**, to enter the colonists' homes at any time and search them for evidence of crimes. Now, our privacy is protected by the Fourth Amendment to the U.S. Constitution. Because of the Fourth Amendment, government officials cannot use general search warrants to search for evidence of crimes. Instead, they can only get a warrant if they first convince a judge that there is good reason to believe specific evidence of a crime will be found in a particular place. Then, if he or she is convinced, the judge issues a specific search warrant "particularly describing the place to be searched, and the persons or things to be seized."

What abuses of privacy led to the Fourth Amendment?

2. Schools keep records on every student. Teachers and counselors write comments about each student in these records. These records are often kept in the principal's or counselor's office. Only teachers, counselors, administrators, or a student's parents may see these records.

3. According to the laws in most states, a lawyer may not, under most circumstances, reveal what a client has said to him or her in private.

4. When Carol's grandfather died, she cried and cried at home. But Carol never let her feelings show at school. When Carol's friends asked her what was bothering her, she just shook her head and didn't say a thing.

Examining Consequences of Privacy

As you can see, privacy may have many different consequences, some of which are benefits and some of which are costs. Some of the most common benefits and costs of privacy are described in the next two sections. As you read these sections of the lesson, think about the benefits and costs that result from privacy in your own life.

Benefits of Privacy

Freedom. Privacy may enable people to be free to think and act as they please without unreasonable and unfair influence or control by others. This freedom may prevent a society from becoming **totalitarian**, that is, subject to complete control by a dictator or ruling party. For example:

- In the privacy of their homes, people may feel free to speak with their family and friends about ideas and beliefs that may not be popular with others. Talking with family and friends may lead to new ideas and thoughts.

How might privacy protect freedom of belief and thought?

Security. If people respect each other's privacy, they can feel secure in their persons, homes, beliefs, and relationships. For example:

- If your friends respect your privacy, you can feel secure that they will not bother you when you want to be alone, or embarrass you by repeating your personal thoughts and opinions to others.

Protection of economic interests. Privacy may enable people to keep to themselves such things as ideas, plans, inventions, and ways of accomplishing goals or making products. This may help them in creating and selling new products and competing with others. For example:

- Suppose you designed a T-shirt that you thought would sell well and make a lot of money for you. Keeping your idea secret until you had created the T-shirts and had them ready for sale would protect your idea from being taken by others.

How might privacy help people protect their plans and ideas?

Individuality. Without privacy, the pressure to be like others might stop an individual from forming his own values, beliefs and opinions. For example:

- Living in a large family or group with no privacy might make someone feel he or she has to go along with whatever the group or its leaders consider correct beliefs and behavior.

How can privacy remove the pressure to conform to others' views?

Creativity. Privacy may be necessary for creative thought or work. For example:

- Suppose you were writing a story, and someone was looking over your shoulder at everything you wrote. You might feel as though you were being judged, or worry about what the person would think of your story. Or suppose people were talking near you or asking you questions. You might find it difficult to concentrate.

How might privacy help people be creative?

Intimacy. Privacy is essential for the development of warm and affectionate relationships with other people. For example:

- People are not likely to develop close friendships and share their innermost thoughts and feelings with others unless they can do so in private.

How can privacy help people develop close friendships?

Critical Thinking Exercise
EXAMINING BENEFITS OF PRIVACY

Work with at least one other person to write answers to the following questions. Include examples of real or imaginary situations to explain or illustrate your ideas.

1. Do you think privacy is really necessary for people to develop close friendships? Why or why not?

2. What pressures to be like other people are found in your school and community? In what way does having privacy free you from those pressures and enable you to develop your own thoughts, feelings, and lifestyle?

3. How would you feel if you did not have a right to privacy in your personal possessions, or if people did not respect your wishes when you wanted to be alone?

4. How does privacy help you to be creative?

Costs of Privacy

Loneliness and alienation. Too much privacy can result in people being cut off from others. It can lead to loneliness and to poor relations with others. For example:

- Suppose a person lived alone and rarely interacted with others. Being alone almost all the time might make the person feel uncomfortable dealing with people.

How might privacy interfere with intellectual growth?

Do you think too much privacy can lead to loneliness?

Loss of stimulation and intellectual growth. People correct errors in their thinking and learn new ideas and ways of doing things by interacting with other people. Too much privacy can result in failure to exchange ideas and to learn from others. For example:

- Suppose a person never discussed his or her thoughts with others. It would be difficult for the person to become aware of errors in his or her thinking. It also would be difficult for the person to learn new ideas, and other people would never benefit from the person's ideas and information.

Misbehavior and lawlessness. Privacy may prevent unlawful behavior from being discovered and punished. For example:

- If there are private places where people are not watched, they can go there to commit crimes or to hide evidence of their crimes.

How might privacy create opportunities for crime?

Financial costs. Maintaining privacy may increase the cost of doing things. For example:

- Building homes with separate rooms to provide privacy costs more than building a single large room.

Lack of Accountability. Privacy enables people to do things that cannot be observed by others. As a result, there may be no way to hold them responsible for wrongdoing. For example:

- If they are not being supervised, people might take shortcuts in doing their work, or cheat on a test, or steal. Other people might never discover what has been done, or there may be no way to prove who is responsible.

Critical Thinking Exercise
EXAMINING COSTS OF PRIVACY

Work with at least one other person to write answers to the following questions. Include examples of real or imaginary situations to explain or illustrate your ideas.

1. Can too much privacy make it difficult to be creative? Explain your answer.

2. How might privacy lead to difficulties in developing friendships and in relating to other people?

3. In what ways does privacy increase the cost of doing things?

4. Do you think privacy makes it possible for people to commit crimes and not get caught? Why or why not?

5. Do you think privacy makes it more difficult to hold people responsible for their actions? Why or why not?

Using the Lesson

1. Identify an issue of privacy in the news media, or make up your own example. Prepare a chart which lists the consequences of maintaining privacy in the situation, and identify these consequences as benefits or costs. Be prepared to explain the issue to your class.

2. Working with your teacher, invite a law-enforcement officer or an attorney to class to discuss their ideas about the benefits and costs of privacy. Prepare a list of questions to ask.

Lesson 7

What Might Be Some of the Benefits and Costs of Confidentiality?

Purpose of Lesson

This lesson provides an opportunity to evaluate the benefits and costs of privacy in a specific situation, and to evaluate the importance of these benefits and costs. When you have completed this lesson, you should be able to identify benefits and costs and use these ideas to evaluate, take, and defend positions on issues of privacy.

Evaluating Benefits and Costs of Privacy

Evaluating the benefits and costs of privacy is important before making decisions about issues of privacy. We need to decide which consequences of privacy are most important to us. Are the benefits more important than the costs? Or do we think the costs outweigh the benefits?

People may disagree about which benefits and costs of protecting privacy in a particular situation are most important. They also may disagree about whether the benefits outweigh the costs. For example, consider a rule that protects the privacy of student lockers. Everyone would agree that the benefits of this rule include protection of the students' right to privacy and protection of their personal property.

Everyone would also agree that the costs of this rule include interference with the school administrators' ability to find illegal drugs, weapons, or other improper things that might be hidden in lockers. Some people might think that the benefits of this rule protecting the students' right to privacy outweigh its costs. Others might think that the costs outweigh the benefits. As you can see, it is important to consider benefits and costs when examining issues regarding privacy.

Critical Thinking Exercise
CRIME AND CONFIDENTIALITY

Read the following story. Then work with a study partner and write your answers to the questions that follow. Be prepared to share your answers with the class.

The School Locker Case

Many students at Milton Junior High School have had things stolen from their lockers over the past several months. Neither the police nor the school security guards have been able to recover any of the stolen goods. Stealing happens almost daily at the school. Everyone talks about who they think might be responsible for the thefts, but no one knows for sure.

One day, Bernard stayed after class to have a talk with Mr. Pitts. Mr. Pitts was Bernard's favorite teacher. He trusted him.

"What can I do for you, Bernard?" asked Mr. Pitts.

"I've got a problem, Mr. Pitts. I need to ask your advice. But you've got to promise you won't tell anybody else what I tell you."

"I promise, Bernard. If a student tells me something in private, I would never repeat it to anyone. You have my word on that."

"Well, that's good, Mr. Pitts, because I've got a big problem. It's about the stealing that has been going on here on campus."

"What do you know about that?" Mr. Pitts had just a trace of concern in his voice.

Bernard looked at the floor for a minute, and swallowed hard before he spoke again.

"Yesterday, I was getting dressed after gym class and I heard a couple of guys talking. They thought they were alone. They are the ones who have been doing the stealing! I heard them say so. In fact, they were talking about which lockers to break into next.

"Right after I heard that, I dropped my gym shoe. I guess I got scared. They were pretty big guys.

They turned around when they heard the sound of my shoe, but I pretended I didn't see them."

"I don't know what to do. I'm afraid if I tell on them, they'll find out and come and get me."

Mr. Pitts looked closely at Bernard. He could see that Bernard was afraid. And he understood why. Bernard knew who was responsible for the stealing. Even if Bernard didn't know their names, he would recognize them if he saw them again. Bernard even might be able to identify them from their school pictures.

Bernard was in a difficult position. Mr. Pitts was in a difficult position, too. It would be a relief to everyone on campus if the stealing were stopped. On the other hand, Mr. Pitts had made a promise that he wouldn't tell anyone what Bernard told him. He hadn't realized when he made that promise just how important Bernard's information was going to be.

For what seemed like ages, Mr. Pitts and Bernard just looked at each other silently. Neither of them could think of a word to say.

Identifying Benefits and Costs

1. List four or five possible consequences of Bernard and Mr. Pitts keeping their secret.

2. Write a "B" next to each consequence you consider to be a benefit and a "C" next to each cost.

3. What do you think Mr. Pitts should do in this situation? What should Bernard do? Use the benefits and costs you have identified in developing your opinions.

Using the Lesson

1. Write a story or draw a picture that describes a time when having privacy was very important to you or to someone you know. Then list the benefits and costs of privacy in the story or picture you created. Finally, decide whether or not the benefits outweighed the costs, and explain why.

2. Conversations between teachers and students, doctors and patients, and lawyers and clients, are usually kept confidential, if not by law then by professional standards. What are some consequences of keeping these conversations confidential? Which of these consequences are benefits, and which are costs? Do you think these conversations should be kept confidential? Why or why not?

Lesson 8

What Might Be Some of the Benefits and Costs of the Government Keeping a Secret?

Purpose of Lesson

This lesson provides an opportunity to examine the benefits and costs of allowing an agency of the federal government to keep secrets. The lesson also asks you to role-play a hearing in which different groups take different positions. When you have finished this lesson, you should be able to explain the usefulness of considering benefits and costs in evaluating, taking, and defending positions on issues of privacy. You should also be able to explain why people in different positions might weigh benefits and costs of privacy differently.

Terms to know

Food and Drug Administration (FDA)
executive branch

Critical Thinking Exercise
EXAMINING GOVERNMENTAL PRIVACY

Read the following story carefully. After you have finished, the class will be divided into four groups to evaluate the consequences of secrecy in the story.

Dream-On Sleeping Tablets

People having trouble sleeping could just walk into the local drugstore and buy a bottle of Dream-On Sleeping Tablets. The Drowsy Drug Company, which produced Dream-On tablets, said that if customers took two pills before going to bed, they were guaranteed a good night's sleep.

When the sleeping pills first appeared in drugstores, they sold very well. People seemed eager to try something which might help them get a good night's rest. But after taking the pills, many people woke up the next morning with a bad headache. Some of them complained to the Food and Drug Administration (FDA).

What are the benefits and costs of keeping FDA investigations secret?

The FDA is an agency of the executive branch of the federal government. The FDA was created to help protect the American people from harmful or useless foods and drugs, and from false advertising. Strict laws have been passed by Congress to protect the American people from these things. It is the responsibility of the FDA to enforce these laws. In order to do this, the FDA conducts scientific tests to determine which foods and drugs might be harmful.

As soon as the FDA began to receive complaints about Dream-On Sleeping Tablets, it began a series of tests to see if the pills were responsible for the headaches.

When the FDA tests a product to determine if it is harmful, it does not tell the public that the particular food or drug is under investigation. One reason that the investigation is kept secret is that people might stop buying the product even though it might turn out that it was not harmful.

After the FDA had been testing Dream-On Sleeping Tables for several months, people began to hear rumors that the FDA was investigating the product. Several people contacted the FDA to try to find out if the rumors were true. But the FDA would not release this information. The FDA said that under federal law, it was not required to inform the public about whether an investigation was in progress.

Role-Playing Different Points of View

After reading the story, your class should be organized into four groups to conduct the following role-playing activity. Each of the four groups should represent one of the following organizations:

- Citizens for Safe Drugs
- The Drowsy Drug Company
- National Association of Drug Store Owners
- The Food and Drug Administration

The first three groups should

1. List the benefits and costs of the FDA's decision to maintain secrecy in the above situation.

2. Decide whether the organization your group represents would support or oppose the FDA's decision.

What arguments can you make to support your group's position?

3. Prepare a brief presentation explaining why the organization your group represents thinks the FDA's decision is right or wrong. If your group supports the FDA's decision, explain why the benefits are more important than the costs. If your group opposes the FDA's decision, explain why the costs are more important than the benefits.

4. Select two or three spokespersons to present the group's position to the FDA.

The students representing The Food and Drug Administration will act as hearing officers. While the other groups are preparing their presentations, they should prepare questions to ask the spokespersons and select a chairperson to conduct the hearing.

After each group has presented its position, the group representing FDA should discuss the best and worst consequences of refusing to disclose to the public the fact that a product is being investigated. The group (or the class) should then vote to uphold or to change the FDA's decision. The class should conclude the activity by discussing the usefulness of considering benefits and costs in taking and defending positions on issues regarding privacy and other subjects.

Using the Lesson

1. Why might people in different positions weigh the benefits and costs of privacy differently?

2. Can you think of any institution (such as a school, hospital, or government agency) that has information about you or your friends that you would not want to be made public? If so, do you approve of this example of institutional secrecy? Explain your position.

3. Review the questions you wrote in your privacy notebook or journal at the end of Lesson 5. What do you think the answers to these questions might be? Write them in your privacy notebook or journal. Then write three or more new questions you now have about privacy.

Unit Four: What Should Be the Scope and Limits of Privacy?

Purpose of Unit

Some of the most important issues we face as citizens involve questions about the scope and limits of privacy. That is, what kinds of things will we allow people to keep private, and when will we require privacy to give way to other values? These issues often arise between individuals or groups wishing to maintain privacy, and others who claim the right to know something being kept private. In some cases, it is reasonable and fair to protect privacy. But in some cases, other values and interests may be more important. In this unit you will learn some intellectual tools—concepts and procedures—which are useful in evaluating, taking, and defending positions on issues of privacy.

Lesson 9

What Intellectual Tools Are Useful in Dealing with Issues of Privacy?

Purpose of Lesson

This lesson will introduce you to some intellectual tools useful in dealing with issues of privacy. You will apply these intellectual tools in examining a conflict between privacy and the need to enforce the law. When you have finished the lesson, you should be able to use these tools in evaluating, taking, and defending positions on issues of privacy.

Terms to Know

legality	values
consent	relevant considerations
interests	Freedom of Information Act
legal obligation	warrant
moral obligation	seizure

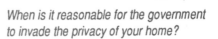

When is it reasonable for the government to invade the privacy of your home?

When should government be able to invade the privacy of your home?

Since colonial times, Americans have believed strongly that citizens should have a right to privacy inside their homes, protecting them from forced entry by government officials. The Fourth Amendment to the United States Constitution (part of the Bill of Rights) prohibits "unreasonable searches" by the government of our "persons, houses, papers, and effects [possessions]." It is not always easy, however, to agree on what is unreasonable.

The Constitution's protection of privacy is not absolute. Government officials are allowed to enter our homes under certain conditions. For example, firefighters may enter our homes to put out a fire. Police may enter our homes to stop a crime in progress or one about to be committed. Police also may enter our homes if they first convince a judge that there is good reason to believe evidence of a crime will be found inside. The judge then issues a search warrant authorizing them to search for that evidence. Government officials also may enter someone's home if the person gives them permission or invites them to come inside.

As you read the following situation, think about the competing values and interests that are at stake, and the choice that must be made between them. Then work with a study partner to answer the questions that follow.

IDENTIFYING CONFLICTING VALUES AND INTERESTS

John Barnes

Imagine the situation of John Barnes. He is a citizen of the United States with all the rights and privileges that go along with that status. Privacy is an important part of his life. It means he is secure in his home. He can cast a secret ballot at election time. He can think about any idea he wants to without fear that the government will try to make him conform to its point of view. But without privacy, his and all other Americans' individuality and freedom would mean very little.

Now add the following facts to our picture of John Barnes. Imagine that Mr. Barnes is suspected of being the leader of a gang of criminals. The police believe that this group has been responsible for the theft of millions of dollars and has injured or killed all those who stood in their way. The police want to put an end to the suspected criminal career of John Barnes. To do so, they need information about his activities. Their job is very difficult because of the right of privacy every person has.

What do *you* think?

1. What values and interests conflict with privacy in the situation described above?

2. Is it necessary sometimes to choose between protecting privacy and protecting other values?

3. Why is it important to have rules or a system for deciding when someone's right to privacy should give way to other values?

Intellectual Tools: Things to Consider in Analyzing Issues of Privacy

As you can see, privacy can interfere with other values and interests that are important. For example, there is often a conflict between the goals of protecting privacy and enforcing the law.

In any given situation, people may have different opinions about how the conflict should be resolved. Following are some **relevant considerations**—things it makes sense to consider, which are important or which might make a difference to us—in deciding how to resolve conflicts about privacy.

- ■ **Consent:** Has someone whose privacy is at issue **consented** to the invasion of his or her privacy? For example, if police want to search someone's home or car, and the person gives them permission to do so, the person has **consented** to the search. Another example would be airport security checks: airline passengers know they will have to pass through a metal detector, and carry-on luggage will be x-rayed, before they can board the plane. Because they know this in advance, and because they could avoid the invasion of their privacy by choosing not to travel by plane, it can be said that they have **consented** to these security procedures. Similarly, elected officials know that much of their personal history and behavior will be revealed to the public.

How can consent justify an invasion of privacy?

Because they could avoid this invasion of their privacy by choosing not to run for public office, it might be said that they have **consented** to the public disclosure of information about themselves.

■ **Legality**: Do those who wish to invade someone's privacy have a **legal right**—a right confirmed by law—to do so? For example, a search warrant issued by a judge gives police a **legal right** to search the places described in the search warrant. Customs officials have a **legal right** to search anyone who crosses the border into the United States. And the **Freedom of Information Act**, a law passed by Congress in 1966, gives people a **legal right** to documents from the federal government, unless the documents contain certain types of confidential or "classified" information.

How can a search warrant justify an invasion of privacy?

■ **Legal obligations.** Does a person have a **legal obligation**—a responsibility imposed or enforced by law—to maintain the privacy of another? For example, certain laws impose a **legal obligation** on doctors and hospitals not to disclose their patients' medical records. Under the Constitution, police have a **legal obligation** not to invade a person's privacy without a warrant, except under certain special circumstances. And if someone signs a contract promising to keep certain information secret, the contract creates a **legal obligation** not to reveal the information.

How can legal obligations require doctors to keep their patients' medical records private?

■ **Moral obligations.** Does a person have a **moral obligation**—a responsibility imposed by principles of right and wrong— to maintain the privacy of another? For example, anyone who promises to keep a secret has a **moral obligation** not to tell the secret to anyone else. Doctors have a **moral obligation** not to reveal private medical information about their patients. Counselors have a **moral obligation** not to reveal what people tell them in private. And lawyers have a **moral obligation** not to reveal confidential information about their clients.

As you read the following case of *Chimel v. California*, think about the considerations listed above. Then work in small groups to answer the questions which follow the case. Later in this lesson your group will use its answers to help decide how the privacy conflicts in the case should be resolved.

Critical Thinking Exercise

EXAMINING RELEVANT CONSIDERATIONS

The Search

Late in the afternoon of September 13, 1965, three police officers arrived at the Santa Ana, California, home of a man named Chimel. The police had a warrant authorizing Mr. Chimel's arrest for the burglary of a coin shop. The officers knocked on the door and identified themselves to Mr. Chimel's wife. They asked if they might come inside. Mrs. Chimel let them into the house. They waited there for ten or fifteen minutes until Mr. Chimel returned home from work. When Mr. Chimel entered the house, one of the officers handed him a warrant for his arrest. The officer asked for permission to "look around." Mr. Chimel objected, but the officers said that they were going to conduct a search anyway. The officers did not have a search warrant authorizing them to search the house.

Accompanied by Chimel's wife, the officers looked through the entire three-bedroom house, including the attic, the garage, and a small workshop. In some rooms the search was quick. In the master bedroom and sewing room, however, the officers told Chimel's wife to open drawers and move things from side to side so that they could see any items that might have come from the burglary. After completing the search, the officers took several items, mainly coins. They also took several medals, tokens, and a few other objects. The entire search took between forty-five minutes and an hour.

What do *you* think?

1. Did Mr. or Mrs. Chimel **consent** to the search of their house by the police? Explain your answer.

2. Did the police have a **legal right** to search the Chimels' house? Why or why not?

3. Did the police have a **legal obligation** not to search the Chimels' house? Why or why not?

4. Did the police have a **moral obligation** not to search the Chimels' house? Why or why not?

How can you evaluate a search of someone's home by police?

Intellectual Tools: A Procedure for Analyzing Issues of Privacy

We have looked at some relevant considerations that can help us think more clearly about issues of privacy. Now we will use these considerations as part of a specific procedure for analyzing issues of privacy. The procedure is a series of steps that you can follow each time you want to evaluate, take, or defend a position on privacy. Please keep in mind that the "person" in each step might be a group or an institution, such as a school or government agency.

1. **Identify the person claiming privacy.** Identify the person who wants privacy and what he or she wants to keep private. How it is to be kept private? What are the reasons for wanting to keep it private?

2. **Identify the persons wishing to invade the other's privacy.** Identify the persons who oppose the first person's claim to privacy. Give the reasons why the claim is opposed. Describe the way in which the first person's privacy is to be invaded.

3. **Examine relevant considerations.** Consider matters that are relevant to or make a difference in conflicts about privacy, such as consent, legality, legal obligations and moral obligations. Determine how these matters apply to the situation.

4. **Evaluate alternative means of managing the issue.** Think about different ways to resolve the issue. These might include recognizing or rejecting the claim to privacy. Or they might involve reaching a compromise. In thinking about these alternatives, be sure to identify and evaluate the costs and benefits of each proposed solution.

5. **Take and defend a position.** Decide which is the best way to resolve the issue and explain the reasons for your decision.

Critical Thinking Exercise
USING INTELLECTUAL TOOLS TO DEVELOP A POSITION

Work in small groups. Apply the five-step procedure for analyzing issues of privacy by answering the following questions about the privacy conflicts in the *Chimel v. California* case. Each group should explain its position to the class.

1. **Identify the person claiming privacy.**

   ■ Whose claim to privacy was endangered in this case?

   ■ What objects might Chimel have wanted to keep private?

   ■ How might Chimel have kept these objects private?

   ■ Why might Chimel have wanted to keep these objects private?

2. **Identify the persons wishing to invade the other's privacy.**

   ■ Who wished to limit or invade Chimel's privacy?

   ■ How did the police limit or invade Chimel's privacy?

   ■ Why did the police want to search Chimel's home?

3. **Examine relevant considerations.**

   ■ Did Mr. or Mrs. Chimel **consent** to the search of their house by the police? Explain your answer.

   ■ Did the police have a **legal right** to search the Chimels' house? Why or why not?

   ■ Did the police have a **legal obligation** not to search the Chimels' house? Why or why not?

   ■ Did the police have a **moral obligation** not to search the Chimels' house? Why or why not?

4. **Evaluate alternative means of managing the issue.**

   ■ What are the costs and benefits of recognizing Chimel's claim of privacy? What are the costs and benefits of rejecting Chimel's claim of privacy?

   ■ What are some other means that the police could have used to gather evidence they needed to prosecute Chimel? What are the benefits of each of these means? What are the costs?

5. **Take and defend a position.**

   ■ What position would you take on the privacy issue in this case? Explain your reasoning.

Using the Lesson

1. If you believe that police never should be allowed to invade people's privacy, then how can society be protected against crime? If you believe that police always should be allowed to invade people's privacy, then how can a person feel secure and be free? If you think that police should be allowed to invade people's privacy only in certain situations, then what rules would you impose on police to tell them when they are allowed to invade someone's privacy?

2. Think about a conflict involving privacy in your school, neighborhood or town. Use what you have learned in this lesson to evaluate this conflict. Imagine alternative ways in which the conflict might be resolved. Decide what is the best way to resolve the conflict. Then explain to the class what the conflict is, what should be done about the conflict, and why.

3. Working with your teacher, invite a person who deals with issues of privacy (such as a police officer, judge, doctor, lawyer, or city council member) to visit your classroom. Ask that person to describe a conflict involving privacy and to suggest several ways in which the conflict could be resolved.

Lesson 10

What Conflicts About Privacy May Arise from Law Enforcement?

Purpose of Lesson

This lesson provides an opportunity to practice using the intellectual tools you have just learned to examine an issue regarding law enforcement. The issue involves the use of hidden cameras to gather evidence on suspected criminals, and the need to protect the privacy of individuals using state parks. When you have completed the lesson, you should be able to use the intellectual tools to take and defend a position on this issue of privacy.

Term to Know

arsonist

Critical Thinking Exercise
APPLYING INTELLECTUAL TOOLS

As you read the following situation, think about how hidden cameras might change people's feelings and behavior. Then work in small groups to answer the questions that follow. Be prepared to explain your answers to the class.

The Eye in the Forest

Almost every year brush fires sweep the hillsides and canyons of Southern California. People's homes are often burned. Sometimes the fires result from natural causes, such as low humidity, dry winds, and lightening. Some fires are not started by natural causes. They are set by **arsonists**—persons who start fires on purpose.

The California Division of Forestry has been experimenting with ways to catch people who illegally set forest and brush fires. One method they've tried is to hide cameras in the forests, focused on stretches of road. Passing cars or people trigger the cameras, which record license numbers and time of day. If a fire breaks out, the pictures give forest rangers valuable clues as to who might be responsible for the blaze. The cameras have only been in use for a short while. State Forestry officials already credit the system with the arrest of one arsonist. They hope that the program can be expanded and eventually turned into a nationwide forest fire prevention system.

But not everyone is so enthusiastic about the new idea. Backpackers, hikers, and bird-watchers go to the forests and mountains to get away from the watchful eye of others. They are concerned that now, even in the forest, their privacy will be invaded. Forest officials say there is no reason for these concerns, because the cameras are only fixed on certain roads. There are no cameras on the trails and meadows in the forest. Besides, the film is only developed and examined when there is a fire. The purpose of the cameras is not to spy on the users of the forest.

Using Intellectual Tools to Develop a Position

1. **Identify the person claiming privacy.**

   - Whose claim to privacy is endangered by the cameras?

   - What might these people want to keep private?

   - How might they keep their whereabouts or actions private?

   - Why might they want to keep their whereabouts or actions private?

2. **Identify the persons wishing to invade the other's privacy.**

   - Who wished to limit or invade the privacy of the people using the forest?

   - How was the privacy of the people using the forest being limited or invaded?

   - What were the reasons for limiting or invading the privacy of the people using the forest?

3. **Examine relevant considerations.**

   - In your opinion, when people choose to use public lands, such as those of the Forestry Division, do they **consent** to being filmed by hidden cameras?

   - Do you think the Forestry Division has a **legal right** to place hidden cameras in the forest?

   - In your opinion, does the Forestry Division have a **legal obligation** not to invade the privacy of the people using the forest, which would prohibit the Division's use of hidden cameras?

   - In your opinion, does the Forestry Division have a **moral obligation** not to invade the privacy of the people using the forest, which would prohibit the Division's use of hidden cameras?

4. **Evaluate alternative solutions.**

   - What are the costs and benefits of allowing the Forestry Division to use hidden cameras? What are the costs and benefits of prohibiting the Forestry Division from using hidden cameras?

   - What are some other means that the Forestry Division could use to gather the information it needs to catch arsonists or to deter them from starting fires? What are the benefits of each of these means? What are the costs?

5. **Take and defend a position.**

   - What position would you take on the privacy conflict in "The Eye in the Forest"? Explain your reasoning.

Using the Lesson

1. Government agencies have used television cameras to monitor public places such as highway rest areas, parking garages and subway stations. What do you think are the best arguments for and against this practice? Do you agree with the government's use of cameras in this way? Write a letter to the editor of a newspaper expressing your opinions.

2. Some schools have used cameras to monitor hallways, outdoor campus

areas, and problem classrooms. What do you think are the best arguments for and against this practice? Do you agree with the school's use of cameras in this way? Write a letter to the school board expressing your opinions.

What arguments can you make for and against the use of cameras to monitor students' behavior at school?

3. Businesses such as banks and stores often have video cameras that tape persons doing business there. Make a chart of the costs and benefits of this practice. What alternatives can you think of for banks and stores to use? What are the costs and benefits of these alternatives? If you wanted to, how could you persuade the stores to stop using the cameras? Present your suggestions to the class.

4. Imagine that some students at your school have been threatening other students in the bathroom, demanding money and beating them up if they do not pay. The victims are afraid to identify the ones who are causing the problems. The principal has announced a plan to remove the doors from the toilet stalls and put cameras in the bathrooms to protect the students' safety. Do you think this is a reasonable solution? Can you think of any better ways to deal with the problem? The principal has scheduled a time when she will listen to students' views and concerns about the plan. Prepare notes to use for presenting your views orally to the principal. Practice your presentation before the class.

Lesson 11

What Conflicts About Privacy May Arise from Attempts by Government to Label People?

Purpose of Lesson

This lesson provides an opportunity to examine issues of privacy that may arise from attempts by government to label people. Your class will role-play a state legislature and debate a proposed law. The proposed law would require people convicted of certain crimes to wear a badge informing everyone of the crime they have committed. When you have finished this lesson you should be able to evaluate different positions on this issue, and be able to take and defend your own position.

How would you feel if you were required by law to wear a label?

Terms to Know

pillories
criminal code
felony
bill
constituent
amend

Labels and Privacy

Many people are proud to wear symbols of their religious faith. But imagine how you would feel if you were *required by law* to wear a label identifying your religion! Fortunately, freedom of speech and freedom of religion are protected by the First Amendment to the Constitution of the United States. These guaranties of the First Amendment would prohibit such a law here. But in Nazi Germany, and in other European countries conquered by the Nazis during World War II, Jews were required to wear a yellow "star of David" to identify themselves as Jews.

Making a person wear a religious symbol interferes with his or her privacy. It also may communicate beliefs the person does not wish to express. But what about a badge or label that simply stated facts about the person? For example, how would you feel if you had to wear a badge that stated your age? Your weight? Would you feel differently if the badge listed the grades from your last report card?

As we have seen, there are similarities and differences in things people want to keep private. People convicted of a crime probably would not want others to know. Even so there have been many examples of efforts to label criminals, both in history and in literature. In the Bible, after Cain kills Abel, a "mark" is placed on him. In Nathanial Hawthorne's novel *The Scarlet Letter*, a woman convicted of adultery (having sex with someone other than one's husband or wife) was required to wear the letter "A" on her clothes to mark her crime. One of the characters in the book even argues that the woman's forehead should have been branded instead. In colonial times, people in this country were punished by being placed in **pillories**— lockable wooden frames which hold a person's head and hands. Pillories typically were located in the town square, so the people being punished were held up to ridicule by the entire community.

How can different forms of punishment invade people's privacy?

Efforts also have been made to label criminals in modern times. After World War II when France was liberated from Nazi rule, French patriots shaved the heads of citizens who had assisted the Nazis. In the United States police chiefs in some towns have circulated photographs of "suspected shoplifters" to local merchants. And in one recent case, when a person convicted of sex crimes against children had finished his prison term, the judge required

him to post a sign outside his front door: "WARNING: Convicted Child Molester."

Labeling people is a controversial issue. Many people feel that it is degrading to the person who is labeled, as well as an invasion of his or her privacy. But some people argue that labeling is a reasonable way for society to discourage people from commiting crimes, and to protect itself from those who do.

As you read the following selection, think about the reasons why people convicted of crimes deserve to have their privacy rights protected. Also think about whether labeling criminals is a fair and reasonable way for society to punish and to protect itself from those who disobey the law. Then work with a study partner to answer the questions that follow.

Critical Thinking Exercise
LABELING CONVICTED CRIMINALS

You and your classmates have been elected to the state legislature. The **criminal code**—laws which define and establish punishment for crimes—is scheduled for review today. A **bill**, or proposed law, has been introduced. The bill would require all persons convicted of a **felony** to wear a badge or label that says: "CONVICTED FELON." A **felony** is a serious crime, usually punishable by a year or more in prison.

Legislators have different opinions about this bill. Some suggest that each person's crime be identified on his or her badge or label. For example, one person's badge might say, "CONVICTED MURDERER" and another's might say, "CONVICTED THIEF." Some argue that only people convicted of certain felonies, such as rape, murder, and drug trafficking, ought to be labeled. But others oppose the bill entirely. They argue that no one, regardless of his or her criminal record, should be treated this way.

Using Intellectual Tools to Develop a Position

1. **Identify the person claiming privacy.**

   - Whose claims to privacy would be endangered by the bill?

   - What might these people want to keep private?

   - How might they keep this information private?

   - Why might they want to keep this information private?

2. **Identify the persons wishing to invade the other's privacy.**

   - If this bill becomes a law, who would invade the privacy of people convicted of crimes?

   - How would the privacy of people convicted of crimes be invaded?

   - What reasons might there be to invade their privacy this way?

3. **Examine relevant considerations.**

   - In your opinion, when people choose to commit crimes, do they **consent** to being labeled as criminals?

   - Do you think the state has a **legal right** to punish criminals by requiring them to wear identifying badges or labels? Why or why not?

   - In your opinion, does the state have a **moral obligation** not to require people convicted of crimes to wear identifying badges or labels?

4. **Evaluate alternative solutions.**

   - What are the costs and benefits of requiring convicted criminals to wear identifying badges or labels? What are the costs and benefits of not requiring convicted criminals to wear identifying badges or labels?

   - What are some other means society could use to punish and protect itself from people who violate the law? What are the benefits of each of these means? What are the costs?

5. **Take and defend a position.**

   - What position would you take on this bill? Explain your reasoning.

Critical Thinking Exercise
ROLE-PLAYING A LEGISLATIVE DEBATE

Now that you have thought about the issues raised by a proposal to require convicted criminals to wear badges or labels, your class will role-play a debate in the state legislature on this subject. Your class should be divided into three groups:

- **Urban legislators.** You represent people in the largest cities in your state, where violent crime (such as murder, rape and robbery) is a serious problem.

- **Suburban legislators.** You represent people in smaller cities and suburbs, where nonviolent crime (such as burglary and car theft) is a serious problem.

- **Rural legislators.** You represent people in small towns and farming areas of your state, where few crimes are committed.

Each group should discuss how their **constituents**—the people they represent— would view the bill. Would their constituents want them to

- support the bill as written?
- oppose the bill entirely?
- **amend** or change the bill?

Once the group has discussed the bill, each student legislator should decide what position he or she will take on the bill. Consider your own views as well as those of your constituents. Be prepared to explain and support your position in a debate about the bill. In the debate, any proposal to amend the bill should be made by a motion, and should be decided by a vote. After the legislature has debated and voted on all proposed amendments, a vote should be taken to support or oppose the bill (as amended).

What position will you take on the bill? Why?

Using the Lesson

1. Suppose your state legislature was considering a law that would require all persons who are infected with the virus that causes AIDS to wear a button that said "WARNING: infected with AIDS." (AIDS is a sexually-transmitted disease for which there is no known cure.) What do you think would be the best arguments for and against this law? Would you favor or oppose it? Why?

2. Students who do well in school often have their names published in the school newsletter on an "honor roll." Is this an invasion of privacy? Would it be an invasion of privacy if students who did poorly at school had their names published in the school newsletter? What is the difference, if any, between these two situations?

3. Do research at your library to find out what happened in one of the following situations:

    ■ when the Nazis required Jews to wear yellow "stars of David" in different countries in Europe during World War II

    ■ when people were identified as "witches" in colonial America

    ■ when Japanese-Americans were considered to be security risks and were required to leave their homes during World War II

    Report what you learn to the class or make a poster or collage illustrating the situation.

Lesson 12

What Privacy Rights Should Groups and Associations Have?

Purpose of Lesson

This lesson provides an opportunity to role-play an argument before the United States Supreme Court in a case involving the privacy rights of groups and associations. When you have finished the lesson, you should be able to evaluate different positions on the issue of group privacy, and be able to take and defend your own position.

Terms to Know

> freedom of association
> constitutional rights
> gender
> unconstitutional
> invalid

Conflicts About Privacy Rights of Groups

How much privacy should a group or association have? Should a group be allowed to keep the identity of its members a secret? Should a group be able to decide for itself who may be a member?

These questions are often answered by examining claims to **freedom of association**—the right to meet with certain people and to exclude others. The Constitution does not mention freedom of association specifically. Freedom of association may be necessary, however, for other **constitutional rights**—rights protected by the Constitution—to be enjoyed. For example, church members must be free to meet with each other in order to exercise their freedom of religion. And as we have seen, there are certain thoughts and beliefs people will tell only to friends in

private. For this reason, freedom of association helps protect freedom of speech.

But sometimes there are good reasons to limit freedom of association. Whether a group's privacy will be protected may depend on the group's purpose, its size, or its other characteristics. If you and some friends form a club, you can decide not to let others join. But if you open a business, the law requires you to deal with all members of the public on equal terms. A political party may have the right to keep the identity of its members a secret, but a street gang may not have that right.

The following selection is based on the Supreme Court's decision in **Roberts v. United States Jaycees** (1984). As you read it, think about the reasons why groups and associations might want to limit who can be a member. Also think about reasons society might have to require some groups to admit everyone who wants to join. Then work in small groups to answer the questions that follow.

Critical Thinking Exercise
EXAMINING GROUP PRIVACY

The United States Jaycees

The United States Jaycees is a national organization which limits its membership to men between the ages of 18 and 35. Any man in this age group is permitted to join. Members can receive training in business skills. They also meet people who can help them succeed in business. Women, and men older than 35, are permitted to join as "associate members," but they cannot vote or hold office in the organization. The Jaycees hold regular meetings. They also sponsor picnics and other activities to raise money for charities.

Why might the government require a group to admit women as members?

Associate members and the general public are usually welcome to attend these events.

The state of Minnesota passed a law prohibiting discrimination against people on the basis of **gender**, or sex. The law was applied to the Jaycees. It required the Jaycees to admit women as members.

The Jaycees sued to have the law declared **unconstitutional**—contrary to the requirements of the Constitution. They claimed that they were a private charitable organization, and that the state had no business interfering with their membership decisions. The law violated their right to freedom of association. Therefore, the law was **invalid**—of no force or effect.

The state of Minnesota did not agree. The state claimed that the Jaycees were a business group. The law was necessary to prevent discrimination against women in business. Therefore, the law was constitutional and valid.

If you were a member of the Supreme Court, what would you decide?

Using Intellectual Tools to Develop a Position

1. **Identify the person claiming privacy.**

   - Whose claim to privacy was endangered in this case?

   - What might the Jaycees have wanted to keep private?

   - Why might the Jaycees have wanted to keep those things private?

2. **Identify the persons wishing to limit or invade the other's privacy.**

   - Who wished to limit or invade the Jaycees' privacy?

   - How was the Jaycees' privacy to be limited or invaded?

   - Why was the Jaycees' privacy to be limited or invaded?

3. **Examine relevant considerations.**

- Do you think the Jaycees **consent** to state regulation of their membership policies by engaging in business-related activities?

- In your opinion, does the state of Minnesota have a **legal right** to prohibit discrimination against people on the basis of gender? What if this limits the Jaycees' freedom of association?

- Does the state of Minnesota have a **legal obligation** not to interfere with the Jaycees' private membership decisions?

- Does the state of Minnesota have a **moral obligation** not to interfere with the Jaycees' private membership decisions?

4. **Evaluate alternative solutions.**

- What are the costs and benefits of recognizing the Jaycees' claims to privacy and freedom of association? What are the costs and benefits of rejecting the Jaycees' claims to privacy and freedom of association?

- What are some other means that the state of Minnesota could use to ensure equal rights for women in the business world? What are the benefits of each of these means? What are the costs?

5. **Take and defend a position.**

- What position would you take on the privacy conflict in this case? Explain your reasoning.

Critical Thinking Exercise
ROLE-PLAYING A SUPREME COURT HEARING

During this activity you will participate in a mock Supreme Court hearing. Nine members of the class should be appointed as members of the Supreme Court. One member of the Court should be selected as Chief Justice, and will act as the presiding officer. The rest of the class should be divided into the following groups:

1. **Minnesota Attorney General's Office.** Your job is to enforce the laws of the State of Minnesota. Prepare arguments to persuade the Supreme Court that the Minnesota law is constitutional and should be upheld.

2. **United States Jaycees.** You claim that the Minnesota law violates your right to privacy and freedom of association. Prepare arguments to persuade the Supreme Court that the Minnesota law is unconstitutional and invalid.

3. **National Association of Women Executives.** Your organization tries to promote the success of women in business. You want to eliminate all discrimination and barriers to equal opportunity. Although you are not a party to the lawsuit, you have been given special permission to present your views to the Court. Prepare arguments to persuade the Supreme Court the Minnesota law is constitutional and should be upheld.

4. **Association of American Golf and Tennis Clubs.** Your organization represents hundreds of private golf and tennis clubs across the United States. The clubs are worried that other states will pass similar

laws if the Minnesota law is upheld. If this happens, their freedom to select and reject members may be limited. You have been given special permission to present your views to the Supreme Court. Prepare arguments to persuade the Court that social clubs should have the right to freedom of association, and the law is unconstitutional because it violates that right.

Each group should decide on the best arguments for its position. Then the group should select two or three "attorneys" to present these arguments to the Supreme Court. While the groups are preparing their arguments, members of the Court should prepare questions to ask the attorneys who make the presentations. Following the presentations, members of the Supreme Court should discuss the case in front of the class. Then they should vote to uphold the law or declare it invalid and explain the reasons for their decision.

Using the Lesson

1. Which of the following groups and associations (if any) do you think should be free to decide for themselves who may be a member? Which should be required to admit anyone who wants to join? Which should be required to admit anyone who meets certain standards or qualifications? Explain your position.

 American Medical Association
 Boy Scouts of America
 Communist Party of the United
   States
 Crown Lanes Bowling League
 Democratic Party of Illinois
 National Association of Women
   Lawyers
 National Press Club
 Riverdale Baptist Church
 Riverdale Bible Study Group
 Riverdale Chess Club
 United States Army

2. Which of the following groups and associations (if any) might want to keep the identity of their members secret? Which ones should be allowed to do so? Why?

 A club you form with your friends
 A street gang
 Alcoholics Anonymous (AA)
 American Civil Liberties Union
   (ACLU)
 American Nazi Party
 Greenpeace
 Ku Klux Klan (KKK)
 League of Women Voters
 National Association for the
   Advancement of Colored
   People (NAACP)
 National Organization for Reform
   of Marijuana Laws (NORML)
 Riverdale Bible Study Group
 Rolling Hills Country Club
 Seattle Science Fiction Fan Club
 Young Republicans

Which groups should be free to decide who may be a member?

Lesson 13

How Do Advances in Technology Threaten Privacy?

Purpose of Lesson

In this lesson you will participate in a simulated public hearing. The hearing concerns a proposal to establish a central computer data bank for the federal government. When you have finished the lesson, you should be able to explain and evaluate different positions on the privacy issues this proposal raises. You also should be able to present and defend your own position.

Terms to Know

data bank
retrieve

How do computers affect privacy?

Computers affect the lives of everyone in our society. Computers are at work keeping track of information and making things more efficient in almost everything we do—from the production of electricity to the production of textbooks; from the use of telephones to the use of credit cards; from the checkout line at the grocery store to the check-cashing line at the bank.

But computers also can present problems for privacy in modern society. They can store information permanently, and they can easily **retrieve**, or locate, the stored information. Perhaps you've never thought about just how much information about you and your family might be stored in a computer's memory, or **data bank**. Every time you

- use your telephone, a computer stores the number you call, the date, and the length of time you talk.

- rent a movie from a video store, a computer stores the name of that movie and the date you rented it.

- use a credit card, a computer stores the date, amount of the purchase, name and location of the store, and a description of what you bought.

- subscribe to a newspaper or magazine, a computer stores your name and address, the name of the newspaper or magazine, and the dates your subscription starts and ends.

- apply for a loan, a computer stores your address and phone number, the name, address and phone number of the place you work, how much money you earn, the value of the property you own, how much money you already owe, and how much you pay on your debts each month.

- apply for health insurance, a computer stores your height, weight, age, medical history, the names and addresses of your doctors, and the kinds of medicine you take.

- apply for car insurance, a computer stores your address, driving record, the make and model of the car you drive, how far you drive to work, and how far you drive each year.

- pay your bills, a computer stores the date and amount of your payment.

Computers also store how much electricity and water you use each month, taxes you pay, your hair color, eye color, and whether you wear glasses.

A detailed picture of your life could be drawn from information about you that is stored in computers. Organizations usually can decide whether they will share the information they have stored in their computers. Several private companies have created large computer data banks. These companies combine information from different sources, such as the forms people fill out when they apply for a loan, or a credit card, or a driver's license. Then they sell the information to businesses that use it to identify people who might buy their products. Information disclosed to one person for one reason may be retrieved by other people and used for other purposes.

Computers make it almost impossible for individuals to control who learns personal information about them. And as time goes by, computers will become more powerful. They will be able to store more information. They will be able to retrieve information more quickly. More people and organizations will use computers. Privacy problems are likely to increase.

As you read the following selection, imagine that Congress is thinking about creating a central government computer data bank. The data bank would combine all the information the government now has about every person in the country. Think about the benefits and costs that would result if a central government data bank were established. Then work with a study partner to answer the questions that follow.

Critical Thinking Exercise
THE CENTRAL GOVERNMENT DATA BANK PROPOSAL

Federal and state governments now use hundreds of separate computers to store and retrieve information. In the federal government alone, computers are used by the FBI, Bureau of the Census, Social Security Administration, Department of Health and Human Services, National Park Service, Department of Justice, Department of Labor, Department of Housing and Urban Development, State Department, Pentagon (Department of Defense), and many other agencies. Each government agency has its own separate data bank.

Several studies have recommended that information contained in these separate computer systems be combined in one central data bank. Information known by one agency would be available to all other agencies throughout the United States.

Government workers would have the information they need at their fingertips. Government programs could be run more efficiently, serving more people and saving taxes. Government policies to improve the economy and reduce unemployment would be based on more information, and they might have a greater chance of success. National health problems or epidemics could be managed better. Government could respond more quickly to natural disasters, such as floods, earthquakes and hurricanes. Law enforcement agencies would find it easier to keep track of people who had been arrested or convicted of crimes in the past. People who cheat on their taxes would be easier to catch. A central data bank could help the government operate more efficiently in many ways.

Because of these benefits, many people think establishing a single federal data bank is a good

How do computers affect everyone's privacy?

idea. But others are opposed. They fear that a central data bank would put everyone's privacy at risk, and they raise a lot of questions:

- Would *any* agency be allowed to use the records of another agency for *any* purpose?

- What kind of information could be put in the data bank?

- What if the information in the records was false?

- How would individuals know what was in their files?

- How could the government prevent illegal use or disclosure of the information by government workers?

These opponents claim that a central data bank would give the government too much power and control over everyone's lives. It would create too many serious dangers from misuse. The idea should be scrapped, they say.

Using Intellectual Tools to Develop a Position

1. **Identify the person claiming privacy.**

- Whose claim to privacy would be endangered by a central data bank operated by the federal government?

- What information might people **not** want to have in a central data bank? Why?

- How could information about individuals be kept private?

2. **Identify the persons wishing to limit or invade the other's privacy.**

- How might a central data bank limit or invade people's privacy?

- Why might the federal government wish to have such a data bank?

3. **Examine relevant considerations.**

- By giving information to one agency of the government, do people **consent** to disclosure of that information to other agencies of the government? Explain your position.

- Do you think the federal government has a **legal right** to collect information about people in a centralized computer data bank? Why or why not?

- In your opinion, would a central data bank violate a **legal obligation** of the federal government to respect the privacy of citizens? Explain your position.

- Do you think a central data bank would violate a **moral obligation** of the federal government to respect the privacy of citizens? Explain your position.

4. **Evaluate alternative solutions.**

- What are the costs and benefits of allowing the federal government to create a central data bank? What are the costs and benefits of prohibiting the federal government from creating a central data bank?

- What are some other means the federal government could use to collect information it needs to enforce laws and carry out government programs? What are the benefits of each of these means? What are the costs?

5. **Take and defend a position.**

- What position would you take on establishing a central government computer data bank? Explain your reasoning.

Critical Thinking Exercise
ROLE-PLAYING A PUBLIC HEARING

During this activity, you will participate in a mock congressional hearing. You will suggest alternative ways of dealing with privacy issues raised by a central government data bank. Your class will be divided into the following groups:

1. **American Association of Computer Manufacturers.** You know that a central government data bank would help businesses which manufacture computers.

2. **Citizens for Greater Efficiency Committee.** Your committee favors any proposal which it believes will reduce taxes and make government more efficient.

3. **Citizens for Privacy Committee.** You believe that a central data bank would interfere with people's privacy.

4. **People United Against Technology.** You think technology is dangerous, because it is becoming too powerful. You oppose technology in general, because you think its dangers outweigh its benefits.

5. **House Committee on Government Use of Data.** You will decide whether or not to create a central data bank. You will listen to all different views because you want to make the best decision you can. You know your constituents are concerned about government waste, but they also value their privacy and freedom.

The first four groups should prepare arguments supporting or opposing the development of a central computer data bank. The arguments should identify and take into account the benefits and costs of a central computer data bank. The arguments also should suggest how the group's position would

- protect the privacy of people, and yet,

- give government a way of retrieving information it needs.

The first four groups should select two or three spokespersons to present their arguments to the Committee on Government Use of Data. While the first four groups develop their arguments, the Committee on Government Use of Data should prepare questions to ask each group's spokespersons. The Committee also should elect a chairperson to conduct the hearing.

After the four groups have presented their arguments, each member of the Committee should vote for or against establishing a central computer data bank, and explain why.

Using the Lesson

1. Imagine that Congress was considering a law that would require everyone to carry a "National I.D. Card" at all times. Each person's card would be numbered. The number would be used whenever a person filled out an official form, such as a tax return, hospital admission form, or an application for a passport, driver's license or government benefits. The number also would be used if the person received a traffic ticket or was arrested. What arguments could you make in favor of this law? What arguments could you make to oppose it? Which arguments do you think are the strongest? Why?

2. Why do you think individuals and groups are willing to testify at public hearings? Think about the groups who have just been represented at your mock congressional hearing.

3. What are the benefits of holding hearings on decisions to be made by the government? What are the costs? Should all government decisions be made only after hearings? Why or why not?

Lesson 14

How Useful Are Written Policies in Dealing with Issues of Privacy?

Purpose of Lesson

This final lesson provides an opportunity for your class to establish a policy. The policy will state how the middle schools and junior high schools in your school district must deal with an issue of privacy. The issue concerns identification of students who have been infected with the virus that causes AIDS. When you have finished the lesson, you should be able to explain and evaluate different positions on this issue. You also should be able to explain the usefulness of establishing a policy to deal with situations that are likely to arise again and again.

Terms to Know

virus
AIDS
HIV
HIV-positive
policy
consensus

Privacy and AIDS

As we have seen, privacy sometimes must give way to other values. In the area of public health there is often a conflict between the individual's right to privacy and society's need to prevent the spread of disease. For example, children are required to have vaccinations or "shots" before enrolling in school to prevent them from getting and spreading diseases caused by certain **viruses**—microscopic germs that multiply once inside a body and cause illness.

AIDS—acquired immunodeficiency syndrome—is a deadly disease caused by the virus **HIV**—human immunodeficiency virus. So far, no cure has been found, and no vaccine has been developed which can prevent you from getting infected. People can be infected with HIV for years without showing any symptoms of disease. The only way to know if a person has the virus is to perform a blood test. If the blood test shows that the person has the virus, the test results are called "positive." People with the virus sometimes are referred to as **"HIV-positive."**

In the late 1980s, schools and communities first confronted the issues created by school-age children who had AIDS or who were HIV-positive. In Kokomo, Indiana, Ryan White, a seventh-grade student with AIDS, was not permitted to enroll in school. Ryan's parents had to file a lawsuit to win the right for him to attend classes. In Swansea, Massachusetts, an eighth-grade student with AIDS named Mark was

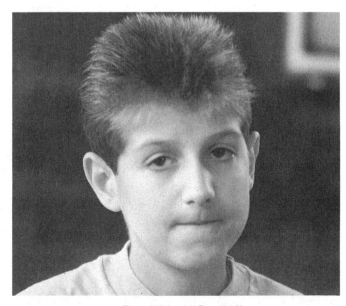

Ryan White (1971–1990)

How would you deal with the privacy needs of students like Ryan?

Why might people with AIDS want to keep their medical condition private?

But in Arcadia, Florida, three brothers with AIDS, Ricky, Robert, and Randy Ray, and their family, were threatened. When the boys attended school despite the threats, someone set fire to their house, and the family had to move to another town.

Threats of violence are not the only reason people with AIDS try to keep that fact a secret. As one teenager with the disease said, "I'm glad people don't know. This way, they treat you as a normal person." In Swansea, Mark's friends and classmates continued to treat him as a normal person, even though they knew he had AIDS. Several explained their support for having Mark in school to a reporter. One pointed out, "It wouldn't feel right if he were home, if he couldn't communicate with his friends. He belongs here. ... He has a right to an education just like we do." Another classmate said, "Think of it [as] if you were in his position—how would you feel?"

Doctors and scientists now know more about AIDS and how the disease is spread. There is no danger of infection with HIV from sitting next to, playing with, or touching someone who has been infected. There is no danger from drinking out of the same cup or water fountain, or from using the same toilet seat. There is no danger from hugging an infected person or even from a simple kiss. You can get AIDS only by getting an HIV-infected person's blood or other bodily fluids in your system. This could happen by having sex with an infected person, or by using a needle that an infected person has used to inject drugs. Before tests were developed to screen out blood infected

with HIV, some people became infected from blood transfusions.

Because of this new knowledge about how AIDS is spread, schools recognize that children with the disease should be allowed to attend class, unless the student is so sick that he or she cannot keep up with the schoolwork. Privacy issues still exist, however. As you read the following selection, think about the reasons teachers and others might have for wanting to know if a student has been infected with HIV. Also think about the reasons the student might have for wanting to keep that information secret. Then work with a study partner to answer the questions that follow.

Critical Thinking Exercise
AIDS IN THE SCHOOL

Nathan and his parents got the bad news in June, right after summer vacation started. Nathan was infected with HIV, the virus that causes AIDS. Dr. Kennedy had been puzzled when Nathan started to lose weight. As an apparently healthy boy who had just turned fourteen, Nathan should have been adding pounds, not losing them. Dr. Kennedy suggested they run some blood tests to try to find a cause. When she told them the results, Nathan and his parents were stunned.

Dr. Kennedy was as supportive as she could be. It was extremely valuable for Nathan, his parents, and Dr. Kennedy to know that Nathan was HIV-positive. By closely monitoring Nathan's health, by making sure Nathan got proper nutrition, rest and exercise, and by using newly developed medicines and treatment procedures, they could prolong Nathan's life.

Later that summer Nathan's parents met with the superintendent of schools, Ron Brown, and told him that Nathan was HIV-positive. Nathan wanted to be treated like any other student, they explained, and they asked Mr. Brown to keep Nathan's medical problem strictly confidential. Mr. Brown assured them that the school system would protect Nathan's privacy as much as possible. No one would be told without good reason. Anyone who was told would be required not to repeat the information. But Mr. Brown could not promise to keep the information entirely to himself.

After Nathan's parents left his office, Mr. Brown considered the issues he would face when Nathan entered eighth grade at Jefferson Middle School that fall:

- Who might need to know that Nathan was HIV-positive? The school principal? Nathan's teachers? His classmates? Their parents? What about other students and teachers at the school? Was there any reason to tell guidance counselors? Did other school employees, such as the school nurse, the custodians, or cafeteria workers, need to know?

- Would it be enough just to say that a student had enrolled who was HIV-positive, or would some people need to be told the student was Nathan?

- How could Mr. Brown make sure that if people were told Nathan was HIV-positive, they would not repeat the information to others? Should people simply be asked not to repeat the information? Should they have to promise not to repeat the information in order to be told? Should some form of punishment be imposed, if they repeated the information without Nathan's permission?

Mr. Brown realized he had a lot to think about before school started.

Using Intellectual Tools to Develop a Position

1. **Identify the persons claiming privacy.**

   - Whose privacy is endangered by disclosure of Nathan's HIV infection?

   - What information might these persons want to keep private?

   - Why might these persons want to keep the information private?

   - How might these persons keep the information private?

2. **Identify the persons wishing to limit or invade the other's privacy.**

   - Who might want to know about Nathan's HIV infection?

   - Why might each of these people want to know about Nathan's HIV infection?

3. **Examine relevant considerations.**

   - Do you think Nathan **consents** to the disclosure of his HIV infection by attending school?

   - In your opinion, do students, teachers, other school employees, or parents have a **legal right** to know which students have been infected with HIV?

   - In your opinion, to what extent does Mr. Brown have a **legal obligation** not to disclose Nathan's HIV infection?

   - In your opinion, to what extent does Mr. Brown have a **moral obligation** not to disclose Nathan's HIV infection?

4. **Evaluate alternative solutions.**

   - What are the costs and benefits of disclosing Nathan's HIV infection? What are the costs and benefits of refusing to disclose Nathan's HIV infection?

- What are some other means students, teachers, school employees and parents could use to be safe from any health risks presented by students infected with HIV? What are the benefits of each of these means? What are the costs?

5. **Take and defend a position.**

   - What position would you take on the privacy conflict in "AIDS in the School"? Explain your reasoning.

Using Policies to Resolve Conflicts

Schools and other institutions often establish a **policy**—a set of guidelines, rules or directions—to deal with issues that come up repeatedly. For example, hospitals usually have a policy about visiting hours, stores usually have a policy about returning merchandise, and schools often have "dress codes," which are policies about the clothes students are permitted to wear.

Policies enable institutions to be consistent in dealing with problems and resolving conflicts. And because institutions often consider different points of view in creating a policy, they

How can dress codes and other policies help institutions be consistent in dealing with problems?

sometimes are able to reach a **consensus**, or general agreement, about how to deal with specific problems when they arise.

Critical Thinking Exercise
ESTABLISHING A SCHOOL POLICY ON PRIVACY

Imagine that the school board has asked your class to recommend a policy for middle schools and junior high schools in your school district to follow in order to protect the privacy of students who have AIDS or who are infected with HIV. The policy should address each of the following issues:

- Who should be told that a student has enrolled who has AIDS or who is HIV-positive?

- Who should be told the student's name?

- What should be done to make sure that people who are told the student's name do not repeat the information to others?

In establishing the policy it is important to make sure that the needs of different people are considered fully. Therefore, the class should be divided into small groups. Each group should be assigned one of the following categories of people, and should evaluate what information the people in that category need to be told about a student who has AIDS or who is infected with HIV:

- **School Administrators** (the principal and other administrators)

- **The Student's Teachers and Guidance Counselor** (all the student's teachers and his or her guidance counselor)

- **Other Teachers and Guidance Counselors** (other teachers and guidance counselors at the school)

- **Other School Employees** (the school nurse, custodians, and cafeteria workers)

- **Students** (the student's classmates and other students at the school)

- **Parents** (parents of the student's classmates and parents of other students at the school)

In order to evaluate how much information is needed by the people in the category assigned to it, each group should

1. List the reasons why the people might need to know the names of students who have AIDS or who are infected with HIV, or might need to know that such a student has enrolled. Each of these reasons will involve some goal or benefit that could be achieved by disclosing the information.

2. Evaluate each reason to determine whether it is truly necessary to reveal the student's name, or the fact that such a student has enrolled, in order to achieve the goal or benefit. That is, can you think of some other way to achieve the goal or benefit that does not require disclosing the information?

3. Consider the privacy interests of the infected student, weigh the importance of the goals or benefits which can be achieved only by disclosing information about the student, and decide whether the people

   - should be told the student's name

   - should only be told that an infected student has enrolled

   - should not be told anything at all

   If the group decides that anyone should be told the student's name, the group also should discuss and decide what should be done to make sure the information is not repeated to others.

4. Select a spokesperson to explain the group's views to the class.

   The class should discuss each group's views and attempt to reach consensus on

   - what information, if any, should be disclosed to the people in each category

- what should be done to make sure that people who are told the student's name do not repeat the information to others

Use a chart similar to the one on the next page to record the class's decisions.

Using the Lesson

1. Suppose Congress was considering a law requiring that everyone in the United States be tested for the AIDS virus. What would be the best arguments for and against such a law? If such a law were passed, what safeguards or limits would you suggest to protect the privacy of each person's test results? Write a letter to your representative in Congress expressing your views.

2. Do you think it is useful to have policies to deal with conflicts about privacy that are likely to arise again and again? Why or why not? Do you think there are also costs or disadvantages to having policies? Explain your answer.

3. Refer to the questions you wrote in your privacy notebook or journal at the end of Lesson 9. What do you think the answers to these questions might be? Write these answers in your notebook or journal. Finally, explain in a paragraph or two what you think are the most important reasons privacy should be protected.

MIDDLE SCHOOL/JUNIOR HIGH SCHOOL POLICY
ON STUDENTS INFECTED WITH HIV

It is the policy of the _____ School
District to protect the privacy of all students to the extent it is reasonably possible to
do so. If a middle school or junior high school student is enrolled who is infected with
HIV or who has AIDS, that information shall not be disclosed except as follows.

The fact that the student has enrolled, but *not* the student's name, may be revealed to the following people:	The fact that the student has enrolled, *and* the name of the student, may be revealed to the following people:

To make sure that people who are told the student's name do not repeat the information
to others without the student's permission, the following measures shall be taken:

RESPONSIBILITY
Table of Contents

Introduction

President Clinton delivers his inaugural address after taking his oath of office as the nation's 42nd president (January 20, 1993)

"Our founders saw themselves in the light of posterity. We can do no less. ... We must do what America does best: offer more opportunity to all and demand more responsibility from all. It is time to break the bad habit of expecting something for nothing, from our government or from each other. Let us all take more responsibility, not only for ourselves and our families but for our communities and our country."

President Clinton's inaugural address, quoted above, calls on each of us to fulfill our responsibilities. But where do our responsibilities come from? How can we decide which responsibilities we should fulfill? And how can we determine who should be considered responsible for an event or situation?

These questions all raise issues of responsibility. Issues of responsibility arise all the time in your day-to-day life.

This study of responsibility will help you gain an understanding of its importance. It also will give you a greater ability to deal effectively with issues of responsibility as they arise in your daily life as a citizen in a free society.

Unit One: What Is the Importance of Responsibility?

Why is it important to fulfill responsibilities?

Purpose of Unit

In this unit we will examine the importance of responsibility to individuals and society. We also will examine where responsibilities come from and what consequences may result from performing and from not performing responsibilities.

LESSON 1

What Is Responsibility?

Purpose of Lesson

This lesson introduces you to the concept of responsibility and its importance in everyday life. You will examine three situations that raise issues of responsibility. You also will examine an issue of responsibility in your own life.

When you have completed this lesson, you should be able to identify responsibilities and to whom they are owed, and identify rewards or penalties associated with specific responsibilities.

Terms to Know

> responsibility
> reward
> penalty
> bill
> constituents
> source

What is responsibility?

As you learned in the introduction, a **responsibility** is a duty or obligation to do something or not to do something. For example, you may have a responsibility to help take care of younger brothers or sisters, to finish your homework before going out with friends, or not to use your parents' tools without their permission. Usually, there are **rewards** or benefits that come from fulfilling responsibilities. If you fail to fulfill a responsibility, a **penalty** or punishment may be imposed. For example, you may receive an allowance if you perform your chores at home, and you may be punished if you fail to perform your chores. As you can see, different consequences result from fulfilling and from not fulfilling responsibilities.

Critical Thinking Exercise
EXAMINING RESPONSIBILITIES

Each of the following situations involves an issue of responsibility. As you read each situation, think about what you would have done if you had been involved. Decide whether or not you would have had a responsibility and, if so, how you could have fulfilled that responsibility. Then anwer the "What do you think?" questions.

1. It was late at night in the city. Most people had finished dinner and gone to bed. Suddenly, a woman's voice was clearly heard pleading, "No! Let me alone!" Lights went on in windows and people appeared looking down on the struggle in the street. A man holding a knife was trying to steal a young woman's purse. "Leave her alone!" someone shouted. The robber looked up to see if anyone was coming and the woman struggled to get free. The neighbors continued to look down as if they were watching television. Seeing that no one was coming to stop him, the robber stabbed the woman and fled with her purse. The wounded woman fell to the ground, bleeding.

2. Mrs. Thompson didn't know what to do. There had been several burglaries in the neighborhood and she thought she knew who had committed them. Just yesterday her son and several of his friends had been watching television at her home. Bob, one of the friends, had been showing off a portable stereo he said someone had given to him. Mrs. Thompson recognized the portable stereo. It belonged to one of her neighbors whose home had been burglarized.

3. Representative Sanchez had to decide how he would vote on a **bill**—a proposed law. The bill would require factories in his district to control air and water pollution. The factory owners would have to spend large amounts of money to do so. This could mean the loss of jobs for some of his **constituents,** the people he represents. They did not want him to support the bill. But other people in his district favored the bill. They would be angry if he voted against it. How he voted could cost him the next election.

What do *you* think?

1. Who has responsibilities in the situation?

2. What are those responsibilities?

3. To whom are the responsibilities owed?

4. Where did the responsibilities come from?

5. What might happen if the person or persons fulfilled the responsibilities? If the person failed to fulfill them?

Why is responsibility important?

In examining and making decisions about a specific responsibility, we need to talk about **why** it is important for people to fulfill their responsibilities. We also need to know something about the **source** of the responsibility—where it comes from. In the next lesson we will examine some common sources of responsibility. First, however, you will examine a responsibility you have in your own life.

What do *you* think?

Think of an important responsibility you have. Then answer the following questions related to it.

1. What is your responsibility?

2. To whom is it owed?

3. What is the source of the responsibility?

4. What are the benefits if you fulfill it?

5. What might happen if you do not fulfill it?

6. Why is this responsibility important?

Using the Lesson

1. Make a chart of the responsibilities you have at home, school, and in your community. The chart should show to whom the responsibility is owed, the source of the responsibility, and any rewards or penalties associated with it.

2. Collect illustrations of responsibility from magazines and newspapers. Use the clippings to create a bulletin board or hallway display.

LESSON 2

What Are Some Sources of Responsibility?

Purpose of Lesson

This lesson provides you with an opportunity to examine several common sources of responsibility. You also will examine different ways people get responsibilities—whether they are freely chosen, imposed by others, or assumed unconsciously.

When you have completed this lesson, you should be able to identify different sources of responsibility and explain how and why people assume specific responsibilities.

Terms to Know

obligation
contract
consent
assignment
appointment
occupation
custom
civic duty
moral principles
conscious choice

Sources of Responsibility

Responsibilities come from a number of sources. The following examples illustrate some common ways people get responsibilities.

1. **Promises:** When an individual makes a promise to another, that person takes on the responsibility or **obligation** of keeping the promises or "living up to his or her word." Sometimes promises people make to each other are in the form of legal agreements which are called **contracts**. At other times, promises are very informal. You should recognize that when you make a promise, you **consent** or agree to fulfill a responsibility or obligation.

   a. Bob borrowed $50 from his friend Clifford to pay for his car repair. He promised to pay Clifford back when he got paid at the end of the week.

   b. Mr. and Mrs. Meyer signed a lease agreement with the landlord to rent the apartment for a year.

2. **Assignments:** Sometimes people **assign** or impose responsibilities on other people.

   a. Mr. Smith assigned his English class the task of reading the first half of the novel by Friday.

b. The school principal assigned the responsibility of keeping order in the lunch room to Mrs. Rodriguez, the sixth grade teacher.

3. **Appointment:** In some situations, people may be chosen or **appointed** to positions that carry responsibilities.

   a. Governor McHugh appointed Wanda Chin to be a justice of the state supreme court.

   b. Coach Castaneda appointed Paul Stockton to be equipment manager for the team.

4. **Occupation:** Each **occupation** or job carries certain responsibilities.

   a. As an automobile repair mechanic, Helen Reed is expected to do a good job fixing cars.

   b. Judge Hastings is responsible for conducting trials fairly, instructing juries properly, and sentencing criminals according to law.

5. **Law:** Laws place responsibilities on almost everyone in society.

   a. Juan Herrera is required to go to school until he is 16 years old or until he graduates from high school.

   b. Part of Jeannette Baker's pay is deducted from her paycheck each week to pay her taxes, as provided by the Federal Tax Code.

6. **Custom:** Some responsibilities come from **customs**—traditions or standard practices that develop over time, which people in society are expected to follow.

a. Joe Wilson stands in line and waits patiently for his turn.

b. Loretta Stern brings a gift to her friend's birthday party.

7. **Citizenship:** In our country, people have certain responsibilities just because they are citizens.

a. Sheri Ricco votes in the election because it is her **civic duty**—an obligation of citizenship.

b. Carlos Jimenez keeps informed about important issues.

8. **Moral Principles:** **Moral principles** are rules or standards of conduct based on principles of right and wrong.

a. Everyone should treat others with respect.

b. Everyone should be fair to others.

Critical Thinking Exercise
EXAMINING RESPONSIBILITIES

Work with a study partner. Answer the following questions. Be prepared to discuss your answers with your class.

1. Identify a responsibility you have which comes from each of the following sources:

- promises
- assignments
- appointments
- occupation
- laws

- custom
- citizenship
- moral principles

2. Of the responsibilities you identified:

    - Which ones did you take on freely or voluntarily?

    - Which were you required to assume?

    - Which did you take on without **conscious choice**—that is, without thinking about them?

3. Of the responsibilities you identified, which two do you think are most important? Why?

4. What rewards might you receive for fulfilling each of these two most important responsibilities? What penalties might you pay for failing to fulfill them?

5. What is the importance of fulfilling these two responsibilities? What might happen if people did not fulfill such responsibilities?

Using the Lesson

1. List one or two of the most important responsibilities other people have toward you. Then answer the following questions for each of the responsibilities:

    - What is the source of the person's responsibility to you?

    - Did the person who has the responsibility take it on voluntarily? Was it imposed on the person? Did the person assume it without conscious thought?

    - What rewards might the person receive for fulfilling his or her responsibility to you?

    - What penalties might the person pay for failing to fulfill his or her responsibility to you?

    - What is the importance of fulfilling the responsibility? What might happen if people did not fulfill such responsibilities?

2. Draw a picture or make a collage to illustrate one of the responsibilities you have and show its source.

LESSON 3

How Can You Examine Responsibilities?

Purpose of Lesson

In this lesson you will learn a set of questions to use when you want to examine responsibilities. You also will apply what you have learned about responsibility to specific situations. When you have finished this lesson, you should be able to use the set of questions it contains to examine responsibilities in different situations.

Terms to Know

warranty
perjury

Responsibility's Rewards and Penalties

Almost all responsibilities have rewards and penalties associated with them. If you fulfill the responsibility of performing a job, for example, one reward is payment for your work. If you fail to fulfill the responsibility of performing your job, however, you might suffer the penalty of being fired. When you are examining a responsibility, it is useful to consider the rewards and penalties associated with a responsibility. The next exercise introduces a study chart you can use to examine responsibilities in a thoughtful and thorough way.

Critical Thinking Exercise
EXAMINING RESPONSIBILITIES

Read each of the following selections and identify the examples of responsibility. Then complete a chart like the one on page 126 for each selection. Be prepared to discuss your answers with your class.

1. **What responsibilities does this warranty or guarantee place on the manufacturer? On the purchaser?**

> **SPINNER HOME DUTY**
> **GRASS TRIMMER Model R 312**
> ## Full Thirty Day Warranty
>
> Spinner guarantees your electric trimmer against defects in materials or workmanship for a period of 30 days from the date of purchase. During the warranty period, Spinner will, at its option, replace a defective electric trimmer with a rebuilt unit, or will repair or replace any defective parts. Just return your electric trimmer to either: (1) the retailer who sold it to you or, (2) any Spinner Appliance Service Dealer. Proof of purchase is required. This warranty gives you specific legal rights, and you also may have other rights which vary from state to state.

2. **What are the responsibilities of the president of the United States?**

The stock market crash of October 1929 marked the beginning of the worst depression in American history. By the time Franklin Delano Roosevelt was elected president in 1932 the economic situation had not improved. During his campaign he had promised a "New Deal" for all Americans. He pledged to create programs to help the jobless, farmers, and other needy groups. He also promised to help improve the outlook for business and industry. Voters who elected him hoped the "New Deal" would start the country on the road to recovery.

What responsibilities did Franklin Delano Roosevelt's campaign promises create?

3. **What are the responsibilities of the judge and witnesses?**

Judge Maria Johnson watched Brian Stone walk toward the witness stand. She had been told that Mr. Stone was likely to be an uncooperative witness. She also knew he had changed his story several times during questioning.

Judge Johnson listened carefully as the bailiff administered the oath to Mr. Stone.

"Do you solemnly swear or affirm that any testimony you may give in this matter now pending before the court will be the truth, the whole truth, and nothing but the truth?"

"I do." replied Mr. Stone.

Judge Johnson thought about her duty as a judge. She was responsible for maintaining order and respect for proceedings and for conducting trials fairly. She said, "Mr. Stone let me remind you that if you fail to testify truthfully under the oath you have just taken, you may be charged with **perjury** (lying under oath). The penalty for perjury in this state is two to four years in the state prison."

4. **What are the responsibilities of the student and employee?**

Jeannette Jackson, a tenth-grader at Drake High School, saw a notice on the school bulletin board.

Jeannette decided to apply for the job after school that day. She needed money to repay a loan her parents had given her to buy a ten-speed bicycle. She hoped the job would take only a couple of hours after school because she needed time to work on her science project. She also wanted to be free on Tuesday afternoons to take piano lessons.

When Jeanette met the store manager, he described the responsibilities of the job. She had to be polite to the customers, help them find things they were looking for, make change, and keep her sales receipts in order and accurate. The hours could be arranged to allow her to be free on Tuesday, but she would have to work from 3:30 p.m. to 6 p.m. on the other days of the week. The manager told her it was very important to be on time, because the person whose place she would be taking each afternoon was a mother who had to be home in time to take care of her young children after school. At the end of the interview, the store manager told Jeannette that she had the job. The pay would be $6.00 per hour.

What responsibilities did Jeannette assume by taking the job?

RESPONSIBILITY STUDY CHART				
Who are the persons that have responsibilities?				
What are the responsibilities?				
To whom are they owed?				
What is their source?				
How were they assumed?				
What rewards and penalties are associated with them?				

Using the Lesson

1. Interview someone who works in your school or community, such as a custodian, a police officer, a coach, a doctor, a teacher, a gardener, or a telephone repair person. Find out what his or her main responsibilities are on the job. Ask what would happen if he or she did not fulfill those responsibilities.

Use the information you gather to fill out a chart similar to the one you used in this lesson. Explain the chart to your class.

2. Draw a cartoon to illustrate a reward a person might receive for fulfilling a responsibility and a penalty he or she might pay for failing to fulfill it.

Unit Two: What Might Be Some Benefits and Costs of Fulfilling Responsibilities?

What might be some benefits and costs of working at the Snack Shack?

Purpose of Unit

When someone fulfills a responsibility, there may be a number of consequences. Some of these consequences may be advantages or **benefits**. In Responsibility Unit One you learned that fulfilling responsibilities may result in various types of **benefits** to an individual. A reward is one type of benefit—there are many other benefits as well.

Sometimes, however, there are disadvantages or **costs** to fulfilling responsibilities. For example, if you assume responsibility for a job, a cost would

be that you would have less time for other activities. In this unit, we will be looking at both the **benefits** and the **costs** of carrying out responsibilities.

It is important to identify the benefits and costs of fulfilling a responsibility in order to decide whether or not to assume that particular responsibility. It also is helpful to identify benefits and costs when deciding which responsibilities are more important to fulfill than others.

LESSON 4

What Are the Consequences of Fulfilling Responsibility?

Purpose of Lesson

This lesson will help you learn to identify the benefits and costs of fulfilling responsibilities. When you have completed the lesson you should be able to explain some of the most common benefits and costs of responsibility. You also should be able to identify the benefits and costs of fulfilling responsibility in a specific situation.

Terms to Know

benefit
predictability
security
efficiency
cost
resentment

Benefits and Costs

There are many possible **benefits** of fulfilling responsibility. Some are benefits to others and some are benefits to the person fulfilling the responsibility.

Benefits to others:

- **Predictability.** When people fulfill their responsibilities, others know what to expect from them.

- **Security.** People feel more **secure** or safe when they know others will fulfill their responsibilities.

- **Efficiency.** Work can be done more **efficiently** or quickly and easily when each person involved fulfills his or her responsibilities.

How can fulfilling responsibilities make life more predictable?

What benefits of fulfilling responsibilities does this cartoon illustrate?

- **Fairness.** If each person does his or her share, it is unlikely that some people will need to do more than their share.

- **Community spirit.** If all members of a group fulfill their responsibilities, it creates a sense of group pride or community spirit.

Benefits to the person fulfilling the responsibility:

- **Independence.** A person with a record of fulfilling responsibilities is more likely to be given freedom to perform with less supervision.

- **Self-esteem.** A person who fulfills responsibilities may gain self-esteem and confidence in his or her abilities.

- **Acceptance and approval.** Persons who fulfill responsibilities are more likely to be accepted and approved of by others, especially by the people who rely upon them.

- **Gains in knowledge, skill, and experience.** Persons who fulfill responsibilities may gain knowledge, skills, and valuable experiences.

- **Increased recognition, status, or payment.** Persons who fulfill responsibilities may gain honors, awards, opportunities for new positions, or increased payment for their services.

There also are several possible **costs** of fulfilling responsibility.

Costs to the person fulfilling the responsibility:

- **Burdens.** Fulfilling responsibilities usually requires time, effort, and/or money.

- **Sacrifice of other interests.** When people accept certain responsibilities, they may have to put aside other interests or needs. For example, they may have less free time for family and friends; or they may be less relaxed and carefree.

- **Resentment.** People may **resent** or feel angry about having to do something they do not want to do.

- **Fear of failure.** People may be afraid they won't be able to fulfill a responsibility or that they will suffer a penalty.

- **Unfairness.** If one person has primary responsibility for a task, it is common for others to let that person do the work and for others not to do their fair share.

Critical Thinking Exercise
EXAMINING CONSEQUENCES OF FULFILLING RESPONSIBILITY

Work with a study partner to review the benefits and costs listed on pages 128 and 129. Select one benefit to others, one benefit to the person performing the responsibility, and one cost. Then describe an incident or example from your own experience to illustrate the benefits and cost you have selected. Be prepared to share your example with your classmates.

Critical Thinking Exercise
IDENTIFYING AND CLASSIFYING CONSEQUENCES OF FULFILLING RESPONSIBILITIES

The story which follows is about responsibilities connected with a particular job. Read the story. Write answers to the questions that follow it. Be prepared to discuss your answers in class.

The Lifeguard

Susan Parker had been working for the county as a lifeguard for almost a month. She still felt a little anxious each morning at 9 o'clock as she climbed her tower eight feet above the warm sand. So far, she had not been required to make any difficult rescues. Even though she had done well in training exercises, she wondered if she would be able to handle the real thing.

Susan liked her job. Besides enjoying being out of doors all day, she felt she was providing important protection to many people. There were days, however, when she wished she could just lie in the sand or go for a swim.

The other lifeguards and her supervisor said she was doing well. Sometimes she worried because she realized that whether or not she did a good job could be a matter of life or death for a swimmer in trouble. This was especially true when the beach was crowded.

What are some benefits and costs of fulfilling the responsibilities of a lifeguard?

Susan thought back to last year when she was an assistant lifeguard. One day a senior lifeguard left his tower without arranging for a backup. A young swimmer got into trouble while the lifeguard was gone. She drowned before anyone could reach her. The lifeguard was extremely upset about what had happened. Since then he has suffered severe feelings of guilt. He was fired from his job, and the county was sued by the girl's family because of his carelessness.

Examining Responsibilities

1. What are Susan's responsibilities as a lifeguard?

2. What might be some consequences of her fulfilling those responsibilities?

3. Which of these consequences are benefits? Which are costs?

Using the Lesson

1. Identify a responsibility you would like to assume. Briefly describe the responsibility and the probable consequences of your fulfilling it. Divide a paper in half. List those consequences that are benefits on one side and those that are costs on the other. Then, number the benefits and costs in order of their importance to you. Explain to your classmates how this exercise might help you make an informed and reasonable decision about whether to take on that responsibility.

2. Interview a person in a job or occupation you find interesting. Ask the person to

   ■ list some of the most important responsibilities of that job or occupation

   ■ describe the consequences of fulfilling those responsibilities

   ■ describe the consequences of not fulfilling those responsibilities

   ■ classify the consequences as benefits and costs, and

   ■ rank the benefits and costs in order of their importance

LESSON 5

How Can You Decide Whether the Benefits of Taking on Certain Responsibilities Outweigh the Costs?

Purpose of Lesson

In this lesson you will role-play a legislative hearing. The hearing concerns a proposal to develop a state park on wilderness land recently donated to the state.

When you have completed this lesson you should be able to use the ideas of benefits and costs in evaluating, taking, and defending positions on issues of responsibility.

Terms to Know

relative importance
public hearing
habitats
agenda
legislative hearing

Evaluating the Relative Importance of Benefits and Costs

As you have learned, there are both benefits and costs to taking on responsibilities. People may have different views about whether the benefits of taking on a particular responsibility outweigh the costs. That is, they may have different views about the **relative importance** of the benefits and costs, or how important one is in relation to the other. Thinking about the relative importance of the benefits and costs of assuming a responsibility can help you decide whether you want to take on the responsibility or not. The following exercise gives you an opportunity to evaluate, take, and defend a position about assuming a particular responsibility by weighing the relative importance of the benefits and costs associated with the responsibility.

Critical Thinking Exercise
WEIGHING BENEFITS AND COSTS

Read the following imaginary situation and the instructions that follow. They will help you prepare to take part in a **public hearing**—a public meeting at which citizens can speak to government officials—on the problem in the story.

The State Park Controversy

A western state recently received a donation from the Thornburg estate of 25,000 acres of wilderness land in a beautiful mountain area near the state capital. A large natural lake is located on the forestland. In the winter the snow is usually several feet deep. The area is perfect for both summer and winter sports.

Representative O'Hara, a member of the state legislature and chairperson of the Committee on Parks and Wildlife, introduced a bill calling for the state to develop and maintain the land as a park. The bill required a large sum of money to develop the park. State taxes would have to be raised to help cover the cost of developing and maintaining the park over the years.

The bill proposes building a small marina on the lake, two campgrounds, a skiing area, fifty miles of hiking and riding trails, and an improved road into the area. These projects would require the removal of a large number of trees and would cause the destruction of some native animal **habitats** (areas animals need to find food and live).

If the legislature supported and voted for the park, jobs would be created. It is estimated that over a hundred government workers would be needed to operate the park. In addition to the people needed to develop the project, the facilities would attract tourists and help the local economy.

All the newspapers in the state covered the story of the proposed park. People began to take sides for and against the bill. The Committee on Parks and Wildlife decided to hold a public hearing to gather information and opinions about the bill. After the hearing the committee will recommend to the legislature whether the bill should be approved or rejected. The committee also can recommend changes in the bill.

People who want to present their opinions for or against the bill have been urged to call the staff of the Committee on Parks and Wildlife and ask for a turn to speak during the hearing. Judging from the number of calls, the room will be full of people wanting to speak. Reporters and others are expected to attend. Each person will be given a copy of the **agenda** (schedule) on the bottom of this page.

Preparing for and Conducting a Legislative Hearing

The agenda or schedule is much like those used throughout our nation in **legislative hearings.** Legislative hearings can be called and conducted by Congress, state legislatures, or local governments. Hearings allow legislators to question experts and other citizens on proposed legislation, and they give people an opportunity to present information and to express their opinions on issues.

To conduct the hearing, your class will be divided into five groups. One group will play the part of legislators on the Committee on Parks and Wildlife. The other groups will represent the organizations listed on the agenda and will testify before the committee. Your class may add other interest groups to the hearing if you wish to create them.

Public Hearing

Date: Monday, September 24
Time: 9:00 a.m.
Location: State Legislature

The Committee on Parks and Wildlife will hear opinions from the public on Representative O'Hara's bill to use state tax money to develop a public park on the Thornburg Estate.

Agenda

1. Opening remarks by Representative O'Hara (2 minutes)

2. Presentations of opinions by interested groups (3 minutes each)
   a. Citizens for Lower Taxes   c. State Ranger's Union
   b. The Wildlife Coalition   d. Citizens for Children's Outdoor Activities

3. Open meeting—questions and answers; comments from the floor (10 minutes)

4. Closing remarks by Representative O'Hara and members of the committee (3 minutes)

5. Adjourn

The major purpose of the hearing is to provide an opportunity for people to express their opinions on the state park bill before the state legislature votes to approve or disapprove it.

Representative O'Hara will serve as the chairperson of the committee. Each of the other groups testifying should follow the instructions in "Developing Group Presentations" and take a stand for or against the bill. They also may suggest changes they believe should be made in the bill.

Developing Group Presentations

Each group (other than the Committee on Parks and Wildlife) should select a chairperson to lead its discussions, a recorder to take notes on ideas to be used in its presentation, and one or two spokespersons to present its position. All group members should be prepared to answer questions asked by the legislators.

In developing their positions, each group should consider the following questions.

1. If the bill were passed, what responsibilities would the state government assume?

2. What would be the probable consequences of the government taking on these responsibilities?

3. Which consequences would be benefits? Which would be costs?

4. From your group's point of view, which benefits or costs would be most important? Why?

5. Does your group recommend approval or disapproval of the bill? What changes, if any, does it suggest? Why?

What arguments can you make to support your group's position?

Group 1—Committee on Parks and Wildlife

Select a chairperson and a recorder. Decide who will take the part of Representative O'Hara. Then review the facts in the case and the procedure outlined on the agenda. Representative O'Hara will chair the public meeting and make sure the agenda is followed.

Your main purpose is to gather information from the testifying groups. Use this information to make a wise decision about whether to recommend the bill as it is, to change it, or to vote against it. Each member of the committee should make a list of questions to ask the representatives of the groups making presentations. All members of the committee should help Representative O'Hara prepare his or her opening remarks.

Group 2—Citizens for Lower Taxes

Your group probably would be against the bill because it would increase taxes. For example, you might argue that the benefits to the public of having the park are outweighed by the cost the public would have to pay to develop and maintain it.

Group 3—The Wildlife Coalition

Some members of your group probably would support the bill because it would preserve the area for wildlife and recreation. For example, you might argue that the benefits to the state's wildlife would outweigh the costs. Others might argue, however, that care should be taken not to spoil the natural environment. You could suggest that the bill be changed to reduce sports activity in the park. This would limit the damage to natural habitats. The area might be used as a wildlife preserve and development might be limited to nature trails and small picnic or camping areas.

Group 4—State Ranger's Union

Your group probably would support the bill because it would add another park to the state system and create new jobs for rangers and their assistants. You could argue that the benefits of having an additional park for people's recreation outweigh the costs of developing and maintaining the park.

Group 5—Citizens for Children's Outdoor Activities

Your group would be for the bill. You might argue that many children in your state, especially those who live in its largest cities, do not have an opportunity to enjoy nature and healthy recreation. If they did, fewer of them might get into trouble or join gangs. You could argue that the benefits to children, their parents and the state far outweigh the costs.

Using the Lesson

1. Working with your teacher, ask a legislator or legislative staff member from your local, state, or federal government to visit your class. Ask your guest to explain public hearings and their usefulness. Ask the person how people in government examine the benefits and costs of various proposals and policies in making decisions. Finally, ask the person to describe the most important responsibilities of his or her position.

2. Working in groups, make a list of at least three responsibilities the president of the United States must fulfill. For each responsibility, make up a list of possible consequences. Which of the consequences are benefits and which are costs? Share your group's findings with the rest of the class by presenting a report, or by preparing an illustrated chart.

3. Arrange to visit a public hearing in your community. Identify the issues involving responsibility and discuss them with your class.

Unit Three: How Should Conflicts Between Competing Responsibilities Be Resolved?

How can you decide which responsibilities to fulfill?

Purpose of Unit

We are often faced with competing responsibilities, values, and interests. We need to be able to make reasonable decisions about which responsibilities we should fulfill and which values and interests we should pursue. In this unit you will use what you have learned so far to assist you in making reasonable decisions. You also will learn some additional intellectual tools to use in evaluating, making, and justifying decisions about competing responsibilities.

LESSON 6

How Should One Choose Among Competing Responsibilities, Values, and Interests?

Purpose of Lesson

In this lesson you will examine situations in which people must make a decision among competing responsibilities, values, and interests.

When you have completed this lesson, you should be able to evaluate, take, and defend positions in situations in which choices must be made among competing responsibilities, interests, and values.

Terms to Know

values
interests

What kinds of conflicts may arise in fulfilling responsibilities?

There are two common types of conflicts that can arise when we have to make choices about fulfilling responsibilities.

1. In some situations, two responsibilities are in conflict and there may not be a way to fulfill both of them, at least not at the same time.

2. In other situations, there is a conflict among responsibilities and other values and interests.

In the following critical thinking exercise you will examine each of these types of situations. But first, we will define the terms **values** and **interests**.

- A **value** is something that you think is worthwhile and important, something that is right or good, that you ought to try to achieve. For example, fairness is a value. So are qualities such as kindness and courage. Other values include honesty, loyalty, friendship, privacy, freedom, and justice.

What values are shown in this picture? What are some of your values?

- An **interest** is something that you want or that you are concerned about, such as free time, good health, or rewards of one kind or another.

Sometimes, if you decide to fulfill a responsibility, you might have to sacrifice one or more of your other values or interests. At another time, you might decide not to fulfill a responsibility because some other value or interest is more important to you.

Critical Thinking Exercise
EXAMINING COMPETING RESPONSIBILITIES, VALUES, AND INTERESTS

Read the following stories and then answer the questions that follow.

■ Last week, Gwen's teacher gave the class a homework assignment due the following Friday. Gwen put off the assignment until the day before it was due. She had to use the library and it would take her most of the afternoon and evening to finish her assignment. On Thursday morning, the basketball coach announced a practice after school. Gwen was not sure what to do. She was the captain of the team and they were counting on her to lead the practice.

■ Roger was permitted to use his mother's car to get to and from band practice, but he was not allowed to drive his friends anywhere. On Friday night, his best friend was stranded after practice because he had lost his bus money. It was late and the buses ran infrequently. Roger called home to ask his mom to make an exception just this one time. There was no answer.

Identifying Competing Responsibilities, Values, and Interests

1. What responsibilities are Gwen and Roger thinking about fulfilling in each situation?

2. What responsibilities are in conflict in these situations? What values and interests are in conflict?

3. **What do *you* think?** What would you decide to do? Why?

Using the Lesson

1. Write a story or draw a picture describing a situation in which a person is faced with competing responsibilities. Explain what the person decides to do and why.

2. Do research to find out about one of the following situations in which a person faced competing responsibilities, values and interests.

   - Muhammed Ali was the first boxer to win the World Boxing Association heavyweight championship three times. During the Vietnam War, he was drafted to serve in the army. He claimed he opposed war on moral grounds and refused to serve.

   - In 1859, John Brown, a northerner who hated slavery, went to Virginia planning to lead the slaves to freedom. He and his men seized a government weapons storehouse and several people were killed.

   - Near the end of World War II, scientists in the United States developed the atomic bomb. As Commander-in-Chief, President Truman had to decide whether or not to use the bomb to try to force Japan to surrender.

Present a report to the class. Describe the situation, explain the competing responsibilities, values, and interests. State what decision was made, and explain why you agree or disagree with the decision.

LESSON 7

How Can You Decide Among Competing Responsibilities?

Purpose of Lesson

This lesson introduces you to several additional intellectual tools useful in making decisions about responsibility. When you have completed the lesson, you should be able to use these ideas in evaluating, taking, and defending positions on issues of responsibility.

Terms to Know

urgency
resources
compromise

Considerations Useful in Deciding Among Competing Responsibilities

At this point in your study of responsibility, you have learned to

- identify responsibilities and their sources
- identify rewards for fulfilling and penalties for not fulfilling responsibilities
- identify the consequences, including both benefits and costs, of fulfilling responsibilities

Each of these intellectual tools is helpful in deciding whether or not to fulfill a particular responsibility. There are some other things to consider, however, that can help you to make decisions about responsibilities.

The six ideas which follow will help you when you have to make a difficult decision about carrying out responsibilities and protecting other values you hold. In the critical thinking exercise,

you will use these intellectual tools to make a decision in an imaginary situation.

1. **Urgency:** When choosing among competing responsibilities, it is important to decide which responsibility is more **urgent**, that is, which one should be fulfilled first.

Example: Lennie thought to himself, "I know there are two things I'm supposed to do tonight—read that story for my English class tomorrow and ...what was the other one?" Suddenly Lennie saw his dog, Max. "Oh," thought Lennie, "I promised my parents to give Max a flea bath. "

- Which responsibility do you think is more urgent? Why?
- What situations can you remember in which you have considered urgency in making a decision about responsibility?

2. **Relative Importance:** How important is each responsibility compared to the others?

Example: The next day, Lennie was riding his bike home from school. As he turned the corner near Mrs. Ferndale's house, he saw two-year-old Walter Ferndale right in his way. The only way to avoid hitting him was to steer the bicycle directly into Mrs. Ferndale's flower garden.

- Which responsibility is more important: to avoid hitting Walter or to avoid running over the flowers? Why?
- What situations can you remember in which you have considered the relative importance of responsibilities in making a decision?

3. **Time Required:** The time required to fulfill a responsibility often is important to consider in determining which responsibility to fulfill.

Example: After Lennie went to Joe's Pizza Parlor, where he had seen a "Help Wanted" sign, he spoke to the manager. The manager said, "We need somebody to work behind the counter from 4 p.m. to 10 p.m. every weekday evening. "I just don't have that much time to work and do all the other things I have to do," said Lennie. "Couldn't I just work from 4 p.m. to 7 p.m.? You could get someone else to work the rest of the time." "Sorry," the manager replied.

- What time was required to fulfill the responsibility of the job? Why was this a problem for Lennie?
- What situations can you remember in which you have considered the time required to fulfill a responsibility in making a decision?

4. **Resources Available:** The fulfillment of some responsibilities may require certain **resources** such as money, equipment, physical strength, or a particular skill. Whether or not you possess the necessary resources can be important in deciding whether to take on a responsibility.

Example: "Of course," the manager of Joe's Pizza Parlor continued, "we do need someone to deliver pizzas in the evenings.

Do you have a car?" "I'm not even old enough to have a license," said Lennie.

- What resource did Lennie lack? How did this affect his decisions about responsibility?

- What situations can you remember in which you have considered the resources required to fulfill a responsibility in making a decision?

5. **Competing Values and Interests:** Consideration of other things you might be interested in doing, or of other values important to you, can be significant when deciding whether to fulfill a responsibility.

Example: Lennie got a job at Leonardo's, another pizza parlor. He worked as a waiter, taking orders from the customers, collecting their money, and cleaning the tables. One day, Lennie's friend, Tom, came into Leonardo's. He ordered a pepperoni pizza, but when it was ready he said to Lennie, "I don't have any money. But I'm really hungry. You're my best friend, Lennie. Please let me have the pizza. I'll bring the money in tomorrow."

- What value or interest was in conflict with Lennie's work responsibilities? What should he do? Why?

- What situations can you remember in which you have considered competing values and interests in making a decision about responsibility?

6. **Alternative Solutions or Compromises:** Sometimes we do not need to decide between competing responsibilities, values, and interests, because we can think of alternative ways to solve a problem.

Example: Lennie told Tom, "Look, I can't let you take the pizza without paying for it. But since you're my friend, I'll loan you the money until tomorrow. I'll put my own money into the cash register today, so that the receipts will balance the orders." "Thanks, Lennie. You're a real friend," said Tom.

- How did Lennie's suggestion solve the problem? What other solutions can you think of?

- What situations can you remember in which you have considered alternative solutions or compromises in making a decision about responsibility?

Use these six ideas to help you make decisions about responsibility:

- urgency
- relative importance
- time required
- resources available
- competing values and interests
- alternative solutions or compromises

In many cases, only two or three of these ideas may be of any importance. But you should consider all six before you decide that any do not apply in a particular situation. That way you can be sure you haven't accidentally overlooked anything.

Critical Thinking Exercise
DECIDING AMONG COMPETING RESPONSIBILITIES

Read the story and then work in small groups to complete the intellectual tool chart on page 144. Be prepared to share your ideas with the rest of the class.

Short of Funds

"Why do these things happen to me?" Stacey Clayton asked herself as she counted out her savings—$100 exactly. Just this morning she found out that her favorite band, Marley's Ghost, was going to perform in concert at the sports arena. Tickets would go on sale tomorrow for $30. The show was expected to sell out in a matter of hours.

The trouble was, last week Stacey promised to loan $100 to her best friend, Nikki, so that she could get her car fixed. Now Nikki needed the money to pay the repair bill and get her car back.

Stacey sat down to make a chart like the one on page 144 to help her reach a decision. After she had answered all the questions on the chart, she asked herself these questions:

- What should I do?
- Why?

What do *you* think?

1. Review the information you have written on the chart. What do you think Stacey should do? Why?

2. Your decision will show that you consider certain values or responsibilities to be more important that others. What are those values and responsibilities?

3. Why might another person, using the same information you have considered, arrive at a different conclusion?

Using the Lesson

1. Read a newspaper or magazine and identify a situation in which a person has faced competing responsibilities, values, and interests. Report your findings to the class.

2. Work with a small group of classmates to perform a skit in which the characters face competing responsibilities, values, and interests, and have limited resources. After presenting the problem ask the audience how they would deal with the situation.

Intellectual Tool Chart For Deciding Among Responsibilities

Note: Sometimes questions 7, 9, 10 or 11 may not be applicable in the situation you are trying to resolve. If this is the case, write "not applicable" or "NA" in the appropriate box.

	RESPONSIBILITY 1:	RESPONSIBILITY 2:
1. What are my responsibilities?		
2. What are their sources?		
3. What are the rewards for fulfilling them?		
4. What are the penalties for not fulfilling them?		
5. What are the benefits of fulfilling them?		
6. What are the costs of fulfilling them?		
7. How urgent are they?		
8. What is their relative importance?		
9. What is the time required to fulfill them?		
10. Do I have the resources needed?		
11. What other values or interests are involved?		
12. What alternative solutions are possible?		

LESSON 8

How Would You Deal With the Conflicting Responsibilities in This Situation?

<table>
<tr><td>

Purpose of Lesson

This lesson provides you with additional practice in examining and taking positions on situations involving conflicting responsibilities.

</td></tr>
</table>

Terms to Know

dilemma
Hippocratic Oath
physician

Resolving a Dilemma

In the last lesson you examined situations in which people could not fulfill all their responsibilities. They had to choose which of the competing responsibilities they would fulfill. But sometimes responsibilities are in direct conflict with each other. That is, in certain situations a person has a responsibility to do something and also has a responsibility **not** to do it. Situations such as this are called **dilemmas**. In the following exercise you will examine a dilemma doctors sometimes face.

For more than 2,000 years, doctors have promised to fulfill the responsibilities set forth in the **Hippocratic Oath**—rules of conduct established by the ancient Greek physician Hippocrates. But, as you will see, sometimes these responsibilities are in conflict with other responsibilities.

How can emergency situations create conflicting responsibilities?

Critical Thinking Exercise
DECIDING AMONG CONFLICTING RESPONSIBILITIES

Read the following story which is based on several actual court cases. Then work with a study partner to answer the questions that follow.

The Emergency

Like most other doctors, Jane Green had taken the Hippocratic Oath. She promised to "follow that (method of treatment) which, according to my ability and judgment, I consider for the benefit of my patients...." Jane had always taken the Hippocratic Oath very seriously in her work at the County Hospital.

One night Dr. Green was on duty in the emergency room. An ambulance brought in a man who had been struck by a car. The man was unconscious. While Dr. Green examined the man, an aide checked the man's wallet for identification. The aide found a card in the wallet with the following statement: "In case of injury to Robert Holbrook, please call his church at (899) 132-5412. Do not give medical treatment." The signature of Robert Holbrook at the bottom of the card matched the signature on his driver's license.

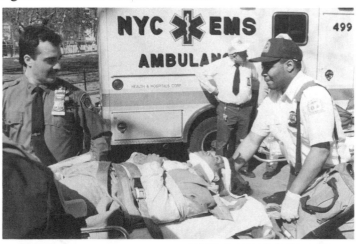

The aide showed the card to Dr. Green. She said, "He's bleeding internally. If we don't operate soon, he'll probably die."

The aide reminded the doctor that the man had signed the card to take care of this very situation. "If he were conscious, he'd be telling us what this card is telling us. He does not want an operation. People who belong to his church believe that medical care interferes with spiritual healing."

"It's my duty to do what I think best for my patients. Get him ready for surgery," Jane replied.

As the aide wheeled Robert out of the room, Dr. Green looked at the card again. She began to wonder if she should follow the instructions on it. For the first time in her medical career she wasn't sure what was the responsible thing to do.

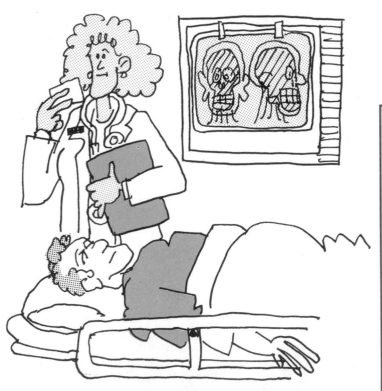

Examining the Situation

1. What are the doctor's responsibilities in this situation?

2. What are the sources of those responsibilities?

3. What might be some rewards for fulfilling the responsibilities? What might be some penalties for not fulfilling the responsibilities?

4. What are the probable consequences of fulfillment? Which are benefits? Which are costs?

5. How urgent is each responsibility?

6. What is the relative importance of each responsibility?

7. What amount of time would be required to fulfill each responsibility?

8. What resources are required to fulfill each responsibility?

9. What other values or interests are involved?

10. What alternative solutions are possible?

11. **What do *you* think?** What should Dr. Green do? Why?

Using the Lesson

1. Working with your teacher, interview a member of the medical profession. Ask that person to describe situations in which he or she has faced conflicting responsibilities. Ask the person to describe what happened, the decision reached, and the reasons for that decision.

2. Think of a time when you or someone you know faced a dilemma. Draw a picture or write a short report to describe the situation. Describe what happened and explain the reasons for the decision that was made.

LESSON 9

Which Responsibilities Should the Representative Fulfill?

Purpose of Lesson

In this lesson you will role-play a situation in which you try to persuade a member of Congress to fulfill certain responsibilities. When you have completed the lesson you should be able to use the intellectual tools you have learned to evaluate, take, and defend positions on how to resolve competing and conflicting responsibilities, values, and interests.

Critical Thinking Exercise
TAKING AND DEFENDING A POSITION

Read the following situation. Then, follow the instructions in the section Developing and Presenting Group Positions.

Should the Air Force Base Be Closed?

Times had changed. The Soviet Union had collapsed. The "cold war" was over. The United States could reduce the size—and cost—of the military. Taxes could be decreased, and money could be spent on other programs.

The military's Base Closure Committee had submitted a list of military bases around the country which were not needed any more. The President had approved the list, and sent it to Congress. Now it was time for Congress to act.

As Representative Martin listened to the debate among other members of the House of Representatives, she was troubled. She knew she was expected to express her opinion and cast her vote on the base closure bill being discussed. But she was faced with competing and even conflicting responsibilities and interests. The bill, if made into law, would eliminate an air force base in the district of another Congressperson in her state, a fellow Democrat.

The air force base was located in the second largest city in the state. It provided more jobs than any other employer in the city. If the base was closed, the city's economy could be devastated. Thousands of people would be put out of work.

Although the air force base was not in her district, Martin had originally opposed the idea of closing it. She had not felt strongly about the issue, nor had her constituents, who lived in a distant part of the state. Her support was partially due to friendship for the Democratic representative from that area, who had made it his top priority to keep the air force base open. It was also the result of her belief that if she were to support her colleague on this issue, her favor would be returned on other matters.

How can elected officials resolve conflicting responsibilities to their constituents?

The issue was receiving a great deal of attention. Representative Martin and other members of Congress were feeling pressure from various groups interested in the outcome. For example, just last week she met with members of the Democratic Club from her community who came to discuss various local matters. The group had provided considerable assistance in her election and, she hoped, would do the same in the next election. In the course of the conversation, the group made it clear that they were in favor of keeping the base open and they expected her to continue to support her fellow Democrat.

As luck would have it, as soon as this group left Representative Martin's office a representative of the Association of Aged and Retired Persons entered. He tried to persuade her to vote in favor of the bill so that taxes could be reduced. Martin had received substantial campaign contributions from members of the Association, and many of her constituents were retired and lived on fixed incomes.

Representative Martin also received visits from

- a group of retired army officers, who insisted that she had an obligation to support the bill because it would make the military more efficient
- the Banker's Association from her district, who took the position that by opposing the bill she would be helping the economy of the state
- people who lived near the air force base who opposed its closure
- people who favored the reduction of defense spending, who supported the bill

She listened to all of them with equal attention.

Faced with these conflicting demands, Representative Martin reflected on her responsibilities. She was responsible not only to her constituents, her supporters, and the other members of her party, but also to the interests of all the people in the state and, for that matter, the nation. There was no

What are the responsibilities of elected officials?

doubt that the potential savings from closing military bases around the country were enormous, and would help the government balance the budget. At the same time, it was clear that closing the air force base would seriously hurt the economy of the second largest city in the state. Taking these and other considerations into account, she, as a member of Congress, was responsible for making the best decision possible. She could not please everyone or fulfill what she saw as conflicting responsibilities to her various constituents, colleagues, and interests.

What arguments can you make to support your group's position?

Developing and Presenting Group Positions

The class should be divided into small groups of students. Each group should be assigned to represent a position similar to one described in the story. One group of three to five students should take the role of Representative Martin and her staff and be prepared to ask questions of the groups making presentations to them.

Each group should prepare its presentation by answering the questions on the chart on page 150. Answer the questions from the point of view assigned to your group. The chart of considerations is provided to help you justify a position among Representative Martin's competing responsibilities. Once presentations have been prepared, groups should take turns presenting them and answering the questions of Representative Martin and her staff.

After role-playing the meeting, talk about your own views on this issue. Your personal opinions might differ from the one you were assigned to present during the exercise.

Using the Lesson

1. Find an article in a newspaper or magazine that describes a situation in which a legislator faced competing responsibilities and had to make a decision. Try to discover the reasoning behind the legislator's decision and be prepared to explain your findings to your class.

2. Working with your teacher, ask a legislator or legislative staff member to visit your class for an interview. Ask the following questions:

   ■ What are some of your most important responsibilities?

   ■ Describe a situation in which you had to make a decision among conflicting responsibilities, values, or interests.

   ■ What considerations did you take into account in reaching your decision?

3. Imagine you are one of Representative Martin's constituents. Write a letter to your representative explaining how you think she should vote and why.

REPRESENTATIVE MARTIN'S CHART OF CONSIDERATIONS

1. What responsibility does the group you represent wish Representative Martin to fulfill?	
2. What might be the **rewards** for fulfilling the responsibility?	
3. What might be the **penalties** for not fulfilling the responsibility?	
4. What is the **source** of the responsibility?	
5. What would be the **benefits** of fulfilling the responsibility?	
6. What would be the **costs** of fulfilling the responsibility?	
7. How **important** is fulfilling this particular responsibility?	
8. What **other interests** and **values** are related to fulfilling this responsibility?	
9. Is there an **alternative** or a compromise **solution**?	
10. What should Representative Martin do? Why?	

Unit Four: Who Should Be Considered Responsible?

Why is it important to decide who should be considered responsible for an event or situation?

Purpose of Unit

In the first three Responsibility units, we have talked about responsibilities as the duties or obligations of a person or persons.

In this unit, we will be using the term "responsibility" in the context of determining the source or cause of an event or situation. The unit will provide you with a set of intellectual tools to use in evaluating and taking positions on when persons should be considered "responsible"—when they deserve the credit or the blame—for an event or situation.

LESSON 10

Why Might We Want to Decide Who Is Responsible?

Purpose of Lesson

In this lesson you will examine reasons people want to be able to determine whether a person is responsible for wrongdoing or for an achievement. You also will examine some of the difficulties of making decisions in complicated situations.

When you have completed the lesson, you should be able to explain some reasons people want to be able to determine responsibility and the difficulties of making such decisions.

Why do we want to be able to determine responsibility?

We often want to decide who is responsible for something in order to

- **reward** a person or persons for a positive act or something good they have done
- **penalize** a person or persons for a wrong or injury that they have caused
- **guide** our own actions in the future

The following examples illustrate reasons for making decisions about who is responsible for something.

1. The captain said that David was responsible for the team's victory in last night's baseball game because he made the hit that scored the winning run.

   The purpose for making such a decision may be to give David a reward or credit of some sort, such as a "most valuable player" trophy.

2. The jury decided that Debbie was responsible for Tom's broken arm, because she purposely pushed him off his bike.

The purpose for making such a decision may be to penalize her by requiring her to pay Tom's medical expenses, or perhaps to suffer some other form of punishment. In this situation, we are saying that Debbie caused Tom's injury by a wrongful act.

3. A committee was assigned to study why ninth grade students in the Elmont School District were reading at a sixth grade level. The committee reported that students were partially responsible because they were not studying enough. The committee also said that school district supervisors were partially responsible because they had not provided remedial programs and specially trained teachers.

   The purpose of such a judgment would be to guide future actions, for example, by directing supervisors to provide remedial programs with specially trained teachers and to make sure students study harder.

Sometimes it is easy to determine who is responsible for an achievement or for wrongdoing. In other situations, finding out who is responsible is not quite so easy. The following exercise illustrates how difficult it can be to decide who should be held responsible.

Critical Thinking Exercise
DECIDING WHO SHOULD BE HELD RESPONSIBLE

Discuss each of the following situations with a study partner. Be prepared to explain your answers to the questions following them.

The Collision

Early one morning Charlotte was driving her small sports car down a narrow residential street. Just then George backed his station wagon out of his driveway into the path of the sports car. He could not see the oncoming car, because a large moving van parked on the street blocked his vision. Charlotte was distracted by a cat running across the road and didn't notice the station wagon until it was too late. The cars crashed.

What do *you* think?

1. Who should be held responsible for this collision?

2. How did you make your decision? What things did you consider?

Parkland

A parkland proposal was on the ballot. It would authorize the state government to purchase, develop, and maintain 275 acres of parkland in the Santa Monica mountains in Southern California.

Many groups supported the measure and made contributions to the campaign fund from their treasuries. They also published editorials in their newsletters asking members to vote for the proposition. Individuals also made financial contributions to the campaign as did certain businesses. Other people, who perhaps could not afford to contribute money, worked in the campaign, going door-to-door, distributing information in shopping centers, and helping with mailings. The campaign director, Marcia Clark, worked eighteen hours a day for six months preceding the election as did the other six people on the full-time staff.

On election day, the turnout was unusually high and the parkland proposal passed with 55% of the vote.

What do *you* think?

1. Who should be considered most responsible for the passage of the parkland proposal? Rank the individuals and groups who contributed, from "most" to "least."

2. How did you make your decision? What things did you consider?

As you can see, in many situations it is difficult to determine who is responsible for an achievement or for wrongdoing. To make thoughtful and reasoned decisions about such situations, it is helpful to use intellectual tools—a set of questions to ask or things to consider in a systematic way. The next lesson introduces you to some intellectual tools to use in making decisions about who is responsible.

Using the Lesson

1. Find examples in newspapers or news-magazines of situations in which it has been decided to hold a person responsible for a wrongdoing or an achievement. Write a brief summary of the situation and explain the reasoning behind the decision.

2. Interview family members or people in your neighborhood. Ask whether they think people should be held responsible for their actions in the following situations. Ask the people you interview to explain their answers. Compare their ideas with yours.

   - Tracy had no money and had not eaten for three days. She went into a grocery store and stole some cheese.

   - Karen believed that Martha was an alien sent from Saturn to kidnap her. To save herself, Karen shot and killed Martha.

   - Adam, a four-year-old, used a garden hose to wash the car. After the outside was clean, he put the hose through the window to clean the inside of the car. The floor mats were ruined and had to be replaced.

LESSON 11

What Intellectual Tools Are Useful in Determining Responsibility?

Purpose of Lesson

This lesson introduces you to a set of intellectual tools useful in deciding when individuals should be considered responsible for an achievement or a wrongdoing. When you have completed this lesson, you should be able to use these intellectual tools in making decisions about responsibility.

Terms to Know

state of mind
intent
recklessness
carelessness
knowledge of probable consequences
control or choice

What intellectual tools are useful in determining responsibility?

Every day people in your school, community, and government face problems of deciding who should be considered responsible for one thing or another. Sometimes such decisions are easy to make, but in certain situations, reaching reasonable and fair decisions can be more difficult.

The following intellectual tools can help you decide in a systematic, thoughtful way who is responsible for something that happened. The first three tools will help you to make reasoned decisions about when persons should be considered responsible for an achievement. All

seven tools should be used when you want to determine responsibility for some wrongdoing.

1. What is the **event** or **situation** for which someone might be considered responsible?

   A good first step in determining responsibility is to identify the event or situation. For example, an event or situation for which you might want to determine responsibility could be

   ■ an automobile accident

   ■ the discovery of a cure for a disease

   ■ the soccer team winning the state championship

   ■ vandalism at a school

2. Who are **the people involved** who might be considered responsible for what happened?

   Once you have identified the event or situation, you can list the people who might be responsible for the event or situation. For example, the people who might be considered responsible for the automobile accident described in Lesson 10 would be

   ■ Charlotte, the driver of the sports car

   ■ George, the driver of the station wagon

   ■ the person who parked the moving van that blocked George's view

   ■ the person who let out the cat that distracted Charlotte

3. How might each person be considered to have **caused** the event or situation?

   Once you have listed all the people who might be considered responsible for an event or situation, you need to evaluate how each person's conduct contributed to or caused the event or situation. That is, was the person's conduct one of the main reasons the event or situation happened? Or would the event or situation have happened even if the person had acted differently? For example, you might say the automobile accident described in Lesson 10 was caused or contributed to by

   - Charlotte, because she did not keep her eyes on the road

   - George, because he backed out of his driveway without making sure the road was clear

   - the person who parked the moving van, because the van blocked George's view of the road

   - the person who let the cat out, because the cat distracted Charlotte's attention

4. Did the person's conduct violate or fail to fulfill a **duty** or **obligation** he or she had?

   Once you have determined how each person's conduct contributed to or caused the event or situation, you should evaluate whether the person had a duty or obligation to act differently. That is, did the person fail to fulfill a duty or obligation and, therefore, was the person guilty of wrongdoing? Or was the person acting within his or her rights? For example, in connection with the automobile accident described in Lesson 10:

   - Charlotte may have violated a duty or obligation, namely, the obligation to drive carefully and safely

   - George violated a duty or obligation, namely, the obligation to yield the right of way when entering a street

   - the person who parked the moving van did not violate a duty or obligation, unless the van was parked illegally or was parked carelessly in a dangerous position

   - the person who let the cat out did not violate a duty or obligation, since cats are not required to be kept inside or on leashes

5. What was the individual's **state of mind** when he or she caused something to happen?

   To answer this question, consider the following points:

   a. **Intent.** Did the person or persons **intentionally** or deliberately cause the event or situation? That is, did they act on purpose? An example would be a driver who purposely runs another car off the road.

   b. **Recklessness.** Was the person who caused the event **reckless**? Recklessness means deliberately ignoring risks of serious harm that are obvious. An example would be speeding at 60 miles per hour down a busy city street.

   c. **Carelessness.** Was the person who caused the event **careless** or **negligent**? Carelessness (or negligence) means not paying sufficient attention to risks of harm or damage that should have been forseen. It is the failure to use reasonable care to avoid injury to yourself or others. An example would be leaving a small child unattended next to a pool or lake.

   d. **Knowledge of probable consequences.** Did the person or persons know (or should they have known) the probable results of their actions? Knowledge of probable consequences means being aware of the sorts of things that are likely to happen as a result of what you do.

Why should we examine state of mind in determining responsibility? A person's state of mind can make a difference in how we evaluate their conduct. Consider the following two examples:

1) Fred caused an automobile accident. Does it make a difference if he crashed into the other car:

   ■ on purpose (acted with intent),

   ■ because he was drunk (acted recklessly), or

   ■ because he failed to notice a stop sign (acted carelessly)?

2) Katrina set fire to the drapes with a cigarette lighter. The entire house burned to the ground. Does it make a difference if she was

   ■ only two years old (acted with no knowledge of probable consequences),

   ■ ten years old, and thought she could put the fire out (acted recklessly with knowledge of probable consequences), or

   ■ thirty years old, and hoped to collect insurance money from the fire (acted intentionally, with knowledge of probable consequences)?

Why is state of mind important in determining responsibility?

6. Did the person or persons have **control** over their own actions? Did they have a **choice** to do something other than what they did?

Without control or choice, a person usually cannot be held responsible for his or her conduct. For example:

■ Juanita walked into the bank to deposit her paycheck. Just then a group of masked robbers came in, robbed the bank, put a gun to Juanita's back, and forced her to drive their getaway car.

■ While walking down the stairs at school, Tom was bumped by George. As Tom fell, he could not avoid hitting Susan who then fell and injured her ankle.

7. Did the person or persons have more **important values, interests,** or **responsibilities** which caused them to act as they did?

Sometimes important values, interests, and responsibilities justify or excuse conduct for which a person might be held responsible. For example:

■ Juan broke down his neighbor's door to save three children from a fire.

■ When the fire broke out in the theater, an usher knocked out a hysterical man who had begun to shout, then calmly directed the audience to leave by the exits.

Critical Thinking Exercise
APPLYING INTELLECTUAL TOOLS TO DETERMINE RESPONSIBILITY

Applying the intellectual tools you have just learned is not always as easy as it might seem. For example, how would you apply them to the following situation to determine who should be considered responsible for the accident?

Mary and her friend Lupe were talking in the lunch line. Just as Tom, who was in line in front of them, received his lunch and turned to leave, Mary bumped Lupe who fell against Tom, who dropped his lunch. Lupe claimed Mary bumped her on purpose. Mary said it was a mistake and that she had slipped. Who should be considered responsible for the accident?

Using the Lesson

1. Working with your teacher, invite an attorney or judge to visit the class and discuss what he or she takes into account in determining responsibility.

2. Working with your teacher, arrange to visit a courtroom to observe a trial. Is the trial an attempt to determine responsibility for an event or situation? What is the event or situation being considered? Which of the following intellectual tools seem to be important in the trial:

   ■ cause
   ■ duty or obligation
   ■ state of mind
   ■ control or choice
   ■ important values, interests and responsibilities

Report your findings to the class.

LESSON 12

Who Should Be Held Responsible for This Accident?

Purpose of Lesson

In the last lesson you examined intellectual tools useful in deciding who should be considered responsible for something in specific situations. This lesson is designed to show how these tools can be applied to determine responsibility in a situation involving several persons.

Critical Thinking Exercise
TAKING POSITIONS ON RESPONSIBILITY

Read the following selection about an injury someone suffered while at work. Then work in small groups to complete the intellectual tool chart on page 161 and prepare a presentation on your group's position concerning which person or persons should be held responsible for the injury to James Olson's arm.

An Accident on the Job

On June 16, James Olson cut his right arm in an accident on his job. He was working with a new table saw at Beamer's Carpentry Shop. He was in the hospital for several weeks. His medical expenses were very high.

After the accident, the health insurance investigator interviewed a number of people at the carpentry shop and collected the following information.

At the time of the accident, James Olson was using the saw to cut eight-foot lengths of redwood. Olson had worked at Beamer's for more than twenty years and he was a skilled saw operator. It was his habit, however, to run the saw without a blade guard. The purpose of the blade guard is to shield the saw operator from the saw blade. A company rule required the blade guard to be used,

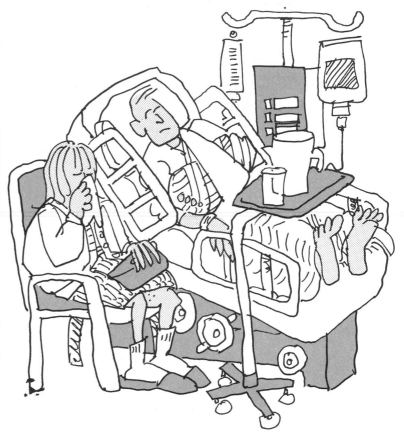

Why might it be important to determine responsibility for an accident?

but Olson claimed the guard just got in his way. He was not using it on the day of the accident.

Nick Greeley is a forklift operator at Beamer's. On the day of the accident, he was operating his forklift next to James Olson's saw. Greeley accidentally backed into the saw causing it to slide toward Olson. Olson was not able to get out of the way in time. Nick Greeley admitted that he had momentarily fallen asleep. He explained that during his lunch hour he had visited his doctor because of a back pain. Greeley had been told that he had been missing too much work lately and he was afraid that he would lose his job. His doctor gave him a muscle relaxant and told him that he should not go back to work because the medication would make him drowsy.

Bill Beamer is the owner and shop manager at Beamer's. He had made the decision to buy this particular saw from Shop Machinery. The saw was delivered with instructions for bolting the table to the floor. Bill Beamer didn't bother to bolt the saw down. He assumed that the weight of the saw alone was enough to hold it steady.

Grace del Campo is an inspector for Shop Machinery. It is her job to follow up on each piece of machinery sold to insure that it has been installed correctly and is working properly. Three days before the accident, Grace was scheduled to check the saw at Beamer's. She was in a hurry that day because she had to catch a plane for her vacation right after work. Since she was only going to be gone a week, she decided to go by Beamer's as soon as she got back. She did not inspect the saw before the accident.

What do *you* think?

1. After carefully considering the information you have put on your chart, who do you think should be held responsible for the injuries to James Olson? Why?

2. Why might it be important to decide who is responsible in this kind of situation?

Using the Lesson

1. Find articles in newspapers about incidents similar to the case in this lesson and report your findings to the class by presenting a study chart you have completed on the incident.

2. Working with your teacher, invite an attorney or judge to class to discuss the case and similar cases.

Intellectual Tool Chart for Deciding Who Is Responsible				
1. What is the **event** or **situation** in question?				
2. Who are the persons who might be considered responsible?	Person 1:	Person 2:	Person 3:	Person 4:
3. How might each person be considered to have **caused** the event or situation?				
4. What **duty** or **obligation**, if any, did the person's conduct violate or fail to fulfill?				
5. What was the person's **state of mind**? Consider: a. Intent b. Recklessness c. Carelessness d. Knowledge of probable consequences				
6. Did the person lack **control**? Could he or she have acted differently? Explain your answer.				
7. What important **values, interests,** or **responsibilities**, if any, excuse the person's conduct?				

LESSON 13

Who Should Be Considered Responsible for This Achievement?

Purpose of Lesson

We often want to decide responsibility in order to punish a person or prevent the person or others from wrongdoing. There are other times, however, when we want to decide responsibility to give recognition or a reward to someone who deserves it. This lesson provides an opportunity to evaluate and take a position on who deserves the credit for an achievement.

Critical Thinking Exercise
DECIDING RESPONSIBILITY

Read the following selection about the construction of a senior citizens' home. Work in small groups to answer the questions which follow.

The Senior Citizen's Home

Maria Azevedo, a student at Hamilton High School, was watching the evening news when she became very upset about a particular story.

"And so," the newscaster said, "there is little hope in sight for the senior citizens of this community. As more low-cost apartment buildings are turned into high-priced condominium projects like this one, more of our older adults on fixed incomes find they have no place to go. The president of the City Council, Jerry Reiner, told Channel 3 news today that the city does not have the funds available to provide these homeless senior citizens with housing they can afford."

That evening, Maria wrote a letter to the school paper. In her letter, she said that the plight of these senior citizens was a disgrace to the community and an injustice to these people who had worked hard all their lives. Maria suggested that if the city government lacked the resources to help, then the students of Hamilton ought to go into the community to find the resources.

When Maria's letter was published, many students were inspired to try to do something about the situation. More than a hundred students gathered at a meeting to discuss what actions they might take. Several working committees were formed. One was given the responsibility of finding out how big the problem really was, that is, how many older adults in the city were homeless. Another committee was put in charge of publicity. The students realized that if they were going to get the community to devote resources to solving this problem, the community had to be more aware of the problem. Another committee was to organize fund-raising activities. Still another committee was to make plans to use money that was raised to solve the senior citizens' housing problem.

During the next two months, the students accomplished a great deal. By interviewing people, including housing experts and older adults, the fact-finding committee determined that housing for about 300 people was required. The committee also learned that these senior citizens could afford an average of $250 a month for rent. The publicity committee did its job, too. Many articles appeared in local papers, and handbills were distributed at movie theaters and shopping centers.

As a result of their efforts, several people offered assistance. Margaret Jones, a real estate developer who had converted many apartment buildings into condominiums, said she felt an obligation to help. She offered to sell some undeveloped property to the city at a greatly reduced price, if it were used to construct low-cost housing for senior citizens. Neal Harns, an architect, offered to donate his services to design the new apartment building.

Funds collected by the students would help pay for some of the materials; the rest would be donated by local businesses. The city agreed to pay for the contractor and equipment. The only piece missing from the puzzle was skilled labor to build the building.

Of course, construction workers could not work without pay for the six months or so it would take to build the building. But they did offer to spend one day a week helping to supervise unskilled laborers, if unskilled laborers could be found.

Then the breakthrough came. Maria Azevedo got a call from the warden at the Ripley State Honor Farm, a minimum security prison. One of the prisoners, Max Davidson, had read about the efforts of the students and others. He had convinced a group of 60 fellow prisoners to offer their services to help construct the building.

A year after Maria Azevedo had seen that first newscast, she herself was interviewed on the TV news at the opening of the White Oak Senior Citizens' Home.

What do *you* think?

1. List all the individuals or groups who might be responsible for this accomplishment.

2. If you were to give an award to the person or group most responsible, to whom would it go? If you were to give awards to the three who were most responsible, to whom would they go? Why?

Using the Lesson

1. Find examples of awards ceremonies in newspapers or magazines. Identify the standards or guidelines that were used in selecting the people to receive the awards.

2. Work with classmates to identify a problem in your community which you would like to help solve. What could you and your fellow students do to publicize and help solve the problem? Make a chart to illustrate your answer.

Lesson 14

Who Should Be Held Responsible for the King's Murder?

Purpose of Lesson

This lesson provides you with the opportunity to apply what you have learned to determine responsibility for a murder in the famous play *Macbeth* by William Shakespeare. The situation calls for you to make a decision using many of the intellectual tools you have studied in this unit.

Critical Thinking Exercise
DECIDING RESPONSIBILITY FOR A MURDER

Read the following story based on the play *Macbeth* by William Shakespeare. Then, work in small groups to answer the questions on the chart on page 167. Be prepared to explain your answers to your class.

William Shakespeare (1564-1616)

The King Is Dead

Early one morning Macbeth, a general in the Scottish army, arrived home after a long journey from the battlefield. He and his troops had been victorious, but something more interesting had happened to him on his trip home, and he was eager to tell his wife. Once inside the castle, Macbeth quickly ran upstairs to his wife's chamber.

"My lady," said Macbeth excitedly. "Listen to my news. On my journey home I chanced to meet three witches. They were very strange women, but they made a fantastic prediction."

Macbeth took a deep breath and continued. "They said that I would become king someday. I've heard that these witches have the power to see into the future, but it is hard for me to believe them. If my cousin, King Duncan, were to die I might inherit the throne. But he is a much younger man than I."

Lady Macbeth listened closely to his story. She was very ambitious. She wanted to be queen. She would stop at nothing to insure that her husband became king. Now she spoke.

"You shall be king, my husband! We are in luck. The king is coming here this very night. We can kill him, and if the witches' predictions are true, you will be named king."

Macbeth hesitated. He didn't like the idea of murder, but his wife had a strong influence on him. Finally, by appealing to his desire to be king, she made Macbeth promise that he would murder Duncan.

That night King Duncan arrived at the castle. After a huge feast, the King went to bed. He told two guards to stand watch outside his sleeping chamber.

Lady Macbeth ran to her husband. "It is time" she cried. "The guards are sleeping." But Macbeth had second thoughts. He praised the king for his kindness. He said he did not want to kill such a good man.

Lady Macbeth urged him on. She questioned his courage. She assured him that the guards would be blamed for the murder. Then she said, "Macbeth! Would you lose your only chance to become king? Go now! Here is the dagger."

Macbeth took the dagger. Stepping over the sleeping guards, he entered the King's chamber. Without further thought, he stabbed the king. When he returned to Lady Macbeth she took the dagger from him. She carried it back down the corridor and placed it near the guards.

The next morning when the crime was discovered, Macbeth and Lady Macbeth acted shocked and grieved. Each suggested that it must have been the guards who killed the king.

What do *you* think?

1. Who should be considered responsible for the murder of the king? If more than one person is responsible, are they equally responsible? Why?

2. Who should not be considered responsible for the murder? Why?

Critical Thinking Exercise
ROLE-PLAYING CRIMINAL DEFENSE ATTORNEYS

Imagine that you are lawyers. Each group should be assigned to represent one of the following persons or groups.

- Macbeth
- Lady Macbeth
- The King's Guards
- The Three Witches

Prepare arguments on behalf of your client(s) concerning their responsibility in the King Duncan murder case. Choose a spokesperson to present your arguments to the rest of the class. After all the groups have made their presentations, use the "What do you think?" questions from the previous exercise to discuss the case.

Using the Lesson

1. Imagine you are Macbeth, Lady Macbeth, or one of the guards. Write a letter to the editor of the Highlanders' newspaper, explaining whether or not you should be held responsible for the murder and why.

2. Read *Macbeth* and act out a scene from the play that deals with or raises issues of responsibility.

3. As a class project, invite an attorney or a judge from your community to discuss a real case which involved a question of whether or not to hold someone responsible for a crime. Ask how the issue of responsibility was decided, and what the reasons for the decision were.

4. Write a short story in which something happens for which one or more persons may be held responsible. Ask your teacher to select two or three of the stories and make a copy of them for each person in the class. Then, working alone or in groups, use the procedure from Lesson 11 to determine who, if anyone, should be held responsible. Discuss your conclusions with other class members.

Intellectual Tool Chart for Deciding Who Is Responsible

1. What is the **event** or **situation** in question?	The murder of King Duncan			
2. Who are the persons who might be considered responsible?	**Person 1:** Macbeth	**Person 2:** Lady Macbeth	**Person 3:** The King's Guards	**Person 4:** The Three Witches
3. How might each person be considered to have **caused** the event or situation?				
4. What **duty** or **obligation**, if any, did the person's conduct violate or fail to fulfill?				
5. What was the person's **state of mind**? Consider: a. Intent b. Recklessness c. Carelessness d. Knowledge of probable consequences				
6. Did the person lack **control**? Could he or she have acted differently? Explain your answer.				
7. What important **values**, **interests**, or **responsibilities**, if any, excuse the person's conduct?				

JUSTICE
Table of Contents

Introduction

Hundreds of thousands of people assemble in front of the Lincoln Memorial during the 1963 Civil Rights March on Washington. Inset: Martin Luther King, Jr. (1929-1968)

"I have a dream that my four little children will one day live in a nation where they will not be judged by the color of their skin, but by the content of their character."

Martin Luther King's speech from the steps of the Lincoln Memorial on August 28, 1963 was a stirring call for justice. His words, quoted above, continue to inspire us; it is almost impossible for a day to go by in which we do not think of something that is just or unjust. Issues of justice arise in our daily lives, in the news media, on entertainment programs, and in the actions of our government and others. The Preamble to the U. S. Constitution states that one of the main purposes of our government is to establish justice in our nation. The Pledge of Allegiance ends with the phrase "with liberty and justice for all."

The central idea of justice is fairness. Despite our belief in justice, it is not always easy to decide what is fair in many situations. In this course of study, you will examine and make decisions about justice in a number of specific situations. In this way, you will learn to apply several sets of "intellectual tools" to different types of problems of justice. These tools will help you deal with issues of justice in a thoughtful, reasoned manner.

Unit One: What Is Justice?

What issues of fairness or justice are shown in these pictures?

Purpose of Unit

Issues of justice can be divided into three categories: **distributive justice**, **corrective justice**, and **procedural justice**. This unit introduces you to these three categories of justice which will be examined in the following units of this program. When you have completed this unit, you should be able to identify issues of justice, and explain why it is useful to do so. You also should be able to identify examples of the issues of distributive, corrective, and procedural justice in your daily life.

LESSON 1

Why Divide Issues of Justice into Three Categories?

Purpose of Lesson

This lesson introduces you to three types of problems or issues of justice, and gives you an opportunity to examine and discuss them. When you have completed the lesson, you should be able to classify issues of justice and explain the usefulness of doing so.

Terms to Know

distributive justice
corrective justice
procedural justice
benefits
burdens

Critical Thinking Exercise
EXAMINING ISSUES OF JUSTICE

Each of the following situations illustrates a different type of issue of justice. For this exercise work in small groups, read and discuss the situations and answer the questions that follow them. Then share your ideas with the rest of the class.

- Suppose you are a member of the basketball team. Your team captain keeps you sitting on the bench and allows his personal friends to play even though some of them do not play as well as you do.

- Suppose you and a friend were walking home from school and you were attacked by members of a gang who beat you up and robbed you. They were arrested, tried, and found guilty, but they were sentenced to probation for six months and did not have to go to jail.

- Suppose someone broke into your school over the weekend and destroyed school property. Although you were not involved, a witness said that one of the persons who broke into the school looked like you. You were called into the principal's office, asked if you had been involved, and questioned about what you had been doing over the weekend. The principal then called your parents and talked to several of your friends, who supported your story. She apologized for taking your time and sent you back to your class.

What do *you* think?

1. What is fair or unfair about each of these situations?

2. What similar experiences have you had or observed?

3. How are each of the situations similar to things that happen in your community?

4. What customs, rules, or laws do you know that are designed to promote justice or fairness in the kinds of situations described above?

5. In the above situations, are the issues of justice similar in any way? Are they different in any way? Explain.

Why divide issues of justice into three categories?

It is useful to divide issues of justice into three types or categories: issues of **distributive justice, corrective justice,** and **procedural justice.** Although this may seem complicated, it is helpful because a different set of ideas or "intellectual tools" is used to deal with each type of issue.

In the next three units you will learn the tools useful in dealing with each type of issue of justice, and practice using them. Before you begin, it is important that you be able to identify the three different types of issues of justice which are explained below.

Distributive Justice: When we are concerned about the fairness of how something is distributed or divided among several people or groups, we are dealing with an issue of **distributive justice**. The thing distributed or divided can be a **benefit**, such as pay for work, or the right to speak or to vote. On the other hand, the thing distributed might be a **burden**, such as taxes or household chores.

How might responses to cheating on a test raise issues of corrective justice?

How might the division of household chores raise an issue of distributive justice?

Corrective Justice: When we are concerned about the fairness of a response to some wrongdoing or an injury, we are dealing with an issue of **corrective justice**. Corrective justice may require a person to give back something that was stolen, pay for damages, or suffer some form of punishment.

Procedural Justice: When we are concerned about the fairness of the **way** information is gathered or the fairness of the **way** a decision is made, we are dealing with an issue of **procedural justice**. Procedural justice deals with the fairness of the procedures or methods used to gather information or make a decision, not with the information or the decision itself.

How might the way trials are conducted raise an issue of procedural justice?

Defining Types of Issues

1. What are the three categories of issues of justice and their definitions?

2. **What do *you* think?** Why should we divide issues of justice this way?

Critical Thinking Exercise
IDENTIFYING TYPES OF ISSUES OF JUSTICE

Work in small groups or with a study partner to complete this exercise. As you read each of the following examples, identify whether it raises an issue of distributive, corrective, or procedural justice. Then answer the questions that follow the examples.

1. After the debate competition, the three students who made the best presentations were given prizes.

2. At the end of the year, the manager of the store gave bonuses to the three employees who had sold the most merchandise.

3. During the early part of our nation's history, several states had laws which restricted the right to vote to white, male citizens who owned property.

4. Our present income tax system is supposed to require people who make more money to pay more taxes than people who make less.

5. Ralph and Susan were made to stay after school for five days to complete homework assignments they had not done.

6. When it was discovered that a late model car had a design flaw that made driving it dangerous, the courts made the manufacturer recall and repair the cars at no cost to the owners.

7. In some countries thieves are punished by death or by having their hands chopped off.

8. If someone carelessly injures another, he or she may have to pay damages for the injured person's medical bills and other expenses. But if the injury was caused on purpose, the person also may have to pay extra damages as punishment.

9. A park supervisor was told that three boys had "roughed up" a younger child. He turned to Sam and his friends and ordered them to leave the park without giving them an opportunity to tell him they had not been in the park at the time of the incident.

10. When Billy was arrested for shoplifting, the judge assigned a lawyer to help him in his trial.

11. Earlier in our nation's history, angry mobs sometimes hanged people without giving them a hearing.

12. Today, before making certain important decisions, boards of education hold public hearings. Anyone interested in being heard on an issue under consideration may attend the hearings and usually may speak at the meeting.

What do *you* think?

1. What is fair or unfair about each situation?

2. What similar situations have you experienced or observed?

Using the Lesson

1. Write a brief description of a situation you have observed or experienced that raised an issue of distributive, corrective, or procedural justice.

2. Watch a television news program and identify reports on issues that involve distributive, corrective, and procedural justice. Describe those issues to your class.

3. Review newspapers and newsmagazines that deal with situations involving distributive, corrective, and procedural justice, and bring clippings from them to class.

Unit Two: What Is Distributive Justice?

What issues of distributive justice do these pictures illustrate?

Purpose of Unit

In Unit One you learned that issues of justice can be divided into three categories: distributive justice, corrective justice, and procedural justice. This unit deals with the issues (or problems) of **distributive justice**, that is, how fairly benefits or burdens are distributed among persons or groups in society.

Benefits may be such things as pay for work or the right to speak or to vote. They may include almost anything that can be distributed among a group of people that would be considered useful or desirable, such as praise, awards, opportunities for education, jobs, membership in organizations, or money. Burdens may include obligations such as doing homework or chores around one's home, working to earn money, paying taxes, or caring for another person. They may include almost anything that can be distributed among a group of people that would be considered undesirable, such as blame or punishment for wrongdoing.

In some situations it can be relatively easy to decide what is fair when a benefit or a burden is being distributed among several people. For example, it is usually considered fair for all students in a class to have the right to take part in a discussion. In other situations, however, fair decisions can be more difficult to make. For example, how good should a student's work be to earn an A, or how much money, if any, should be taken from people who earn moderate incomes to help support people who need help?

Some of the most difficult problems we face in our daily lives have to do with distributive justice. This unit is designed to help you increase the knowledge and skills that will be useful to you in dealing with such issues. It provides you with a set of intellectual tools to help you examine issues of distributive justice and take reasoned positions on those issues.

LESSON 2

What Intellectual Tools Are Useful in Examining Issues of Distributive Justice?

Purpose of Lesson

This lesson introduces you to a set of intellectual tools helpful in dealing with issues of distributive justice. When you have completed this lesson, you should be able to use these tools and explain how they are useful.

Terms to Know

intellectual tools
principle of similarity
need
capacity
desert

What is the principle of similarity?

Once you have identified an issue of distributive justice, there are several **intellectual tools**—ideas or things to consider—that are useful in examining and making decisions about the issue. The first of these tools is a rule which we will call the **principle of similarity**. This principle means that, in a particular situation, people who are similar in certain important ways should be treated alike. In the same situation, people who are different in certain important ways should be treated differently.

An example will illustrate how this principle can be applied. Suppose there was a situation in which ten people were stranded on an island. Three of the ten were equally sick, and there was a limited

Why is need important in deciding how medicine should be distributed?

amount of medicine which they needed to get well. The three sick people are similar in an important way—**need**. They all have the same or a similar need for the medicine, so it would be fair to give each an equal amount. In this situation, the seven other people are different from the three sick people in an important way. They do not **need** the medicine, so it would be fair to treat them differently from the sick people and not give them any medicine.

How are the ideas of need, capacity, and desert used with the principle of similarity?

In the situation just described, we looked at similarities and differences among people in terms of their **needs**. In other situations, we may look at similarities and differences among people in terms of their **capacities**, or abilities. We also may look at similarities and differences among people in terms of **desert**—that is, whether they have earned or deserve the benefit or burden being distributed. One or more of these intellectual tools—**need, capacity,** and **desert**—should be used when we apply the principle of similarity to decide what is fair. These tools will be studied in more detail in the next lesson. First, let's look at some situations involving distributive justice and see how the principle of similarity and ideas of need, capacity, and desert might be used to examine them.

Critical Thinking Exercise
IDENTIFYING AND EVALUATING THE USE OF THE PRINCIPLE OF SIMILARITY

As you read how things were distributed in each of the following imaginary situations, try to identify how the principle of similarity and considerations of need, capacity, and desert were used in making the distributions. Then, for each situation, answer the questions that follow.

1. Only people with the least talent, or capacity, were allowed to become students at the Academy of Musical Arts. The reasoning was that those people had the greatest need to learn.

2. On the island of Exuma, food was distributed to people based on how tall they were. Tall people got more than short people. The reasoning behind this policy was that the shorter a person was, the smaller his or her stomach was and the less food he or she needed.

3. In Carson City, the government used tax money to pay for child care for working parents who needed assistance. The city did not pay for child care for people who did not work or who could afford to pay for it themselves.

Why might the government pay the costs of child care only for working parents who could not afford it themselves?

4. In a planned community, lakeside houses were desired by many people but they were limited in number. To be eligible to buy a lakeside home, people had to be excellent swimmers, own boats, and have received outstanding citizen awards from the city council. It was claimed that these people could use the lake to best advantage, and that because they were outstanding citizens they had earned and deserved the privilege of living in the lakeside homes.

5. In the city of Ribbon Falls, only people under eighteen years old were allowed to vote because it was believed older people were too set in their ways and would never vote for progress.

6. At the state employment agency, jobs were given to people with the most children, regardless of their abilities, because these people needed money to support their children.

7. At the Woodland medical clinic, people were given medical treatment on a first-come, first-served basis, no matter how great their need was for medical treatment.

Identifying Uses of the Principle of Similarity

1. What benefit or burden was being distributed in each of the situations?

2. Explain how the principle of similarity and the ideas of need, capacity, or desert were used to determine who received the benefits or burdens.

3. **What do *you* think?** Do you agree or disagree with the way benefits and burdens were distributed in each of the several situations? Why?

Using the Lesson

1. Identify an issue of distributive justice in a newspaper or newsmagazine. Try to determine how the ideas of need, capacity, or desert were used in dealing with the issue. Be prepared to discuss the issue with your class.

2. Think of an issue of distributive justice in your home, school, or community. Use the intellectual tools you have learned in this lesson to take a position on how this issue should be resolved. Explain your position on the issue to the class.

3. How should the burden of paying for a new public park be distributed among members of a community? Justify your position.

LESSON 3

How Can Intellectual Tools Be Used in Examining Issues of Distributive Justice?

Purpose of Lesson

This lesson helps you learn to use the ideas of need, capacity, and desert in applying the principle of similarity to problems of distributive justice. You also will learn to take values and interests other than justice into account in making decisions.

When you have completed this lesson, you should be able to use the intellectual tools and take other values and interests into account in making decisions about issues of distributive justice.

Terms to Know

irrelevant
values
interests

Using the Principle of Similarity

The principle of similarity states that people who are similar in important ways should be treated similarly and people who are different in important ways should be treated differently. But how do we know which similarities and differences are important in a particular situation? As we saw in the last lesson, decisions based on similarities and differences that are **irrelevant**—unimportant or beside the point—are usually unfair. But when used properly, the principle of similarity and the ideas of need, capacity, and desert form a set of intellectual tools that can be useful in dealing with issues of distributive justice. In this lesson we will look more carefully at the ideas of need, capacity, and desert and at how they can be used in particular situations.

EXAMINING NEED, CAPACITY, AND DESERT

Work alone or with a study partner. Read the sections below that define and explain how the ideas of need, capacity and desert can be used. Answer the questions in the exercise. Be prepared to explain your answers to the class.

1. **Need**

   Consider the degree to which the persons or groups described are similar or different in terms of their **need** for whatever is being distributed.

   For example: Suppose there are ten people waiting in a hospital emergency room. Six have been waiting a long time, but are not seriously injured. The other four, who just arrived, suffered severe injuries in a car crash.

How is the idea of need useful in making fair decisions?

Application of the principle of similarity and consideration of need:

a. Who should be treated first? Why?

b. How is consideration of need useful in applying the principle of similarity to make the decision?

2. Capacity

Consider the degree to which the persons or groups described are similar or different in terms of their **capacity** to deal with whatever is being distributed.

For example: Suppose you could give five children the opportunity to go to summer camp. There are two eight-year-olds, three ten-year-olds, and one two-year-old who wish to go.

Application of the principle of similarity and consideration of capacity:

a. Who should be given the opportunity to go to camp? Why?

b. How is consideration of capacity useful in applying the principle of similarity to make the decision?

How is the idea of capacity useful in making fair decisions?

3. Desert

Consider the degree to which the persons or groups described are similar or different in terms of **deserving** whatever is being distributed. Do similarities in the conduct or status (position) of the persons or groups justify similar treatment? Or do differences in their conduct or status justify different treatment?

For example: Suppose that in the Olympic Games six nations had teams running the 400-meter relay race. At various stages of the race, different teams were ahead, but at the finish the runner from Germany was first over the line, the runner from Canada was second over the line and the runner from the United States was third over the line.

How is the idea of desert useful in making fair decisions?

Application of the principle of similarity and consideration of desert:

a. Which teams should receive the Gold Medal, the Silver Medal, and the Bronze Medal? Why?

b. How is consideration of desert useful in applying the principle of similarity to make the decision?

For example: Suppose ten people show up to vote on election day. Four men and four women are adult citizens who have registered to vote. One is a fourteen-year-old citizen who is too young to register, and one is a twenty-five-year-old visitor from another country.

Application of the principle of similarity and consideration of desert:

a. Who should be given the right to vote? Why?

b. How is consideration of desert useful in applying the principle of similarity to make the decision?

What do *you* think?

1. What situations can you describe from your own experience in which the considerations of need, capacity and desert were important in making a fair decision regarding the distribution of a benefit or a burden?

2. Which of the ideas (need, capacity, or desert) seems most useful in the distribution of the following?

   ■ Driver's licenses
   ■ Membership on a team
   ■ The right to vote in school elections
   ■ Taxes to pay for schools and other services of government
   ■ Punishment for breaking school rules

3. Suppose 100 students were to apply for 25 openings in the school band. What ideas (need, capacity, or desert) should be used to determine who should be selected? Why?

Taking Other Values and Interests into Account

Deciding what would be just or fair is important in many situations. Before taking action on a decision regarding what would be just, however,

it is often reasonable to take **values** and **interests** other than justice into account. A **value** is something that you think is worthwhile and important, something that is right or good, that you ought to try to achieve. For example, fairness is a value. So are qualities such as kindness and courage. Responsibility is another value. Other values are honesty, loyalty, friendship, privacy, freedom, and justice. An **interest** is something that you want or that you are concerned about, such as free time, good health, or rewards of one kind or another.

Critical Thinking Exercise
WEIGHING JUSTICE AGAINST CONFLICTING VALUES AND INTERESTS

Work in small groups to examine the following situation. Answer the questions which follow. Be prepared to explain your answer to the class.

A Disastrous Flood

Year after year the citizens of Gila Bend, a small community located near the Gila River in Arizona, voted against increasing their taxes to repair and to build barriers to protect their

Why might it be important to consider other values and interests as well as fairness in making decisions?

community from floods. Most of the people voted this way because the river had not been known to overflow its banks for over 100 years. During a particularly rainy season, the river overflowed and flooded the community. Most of the homes, businesses, schools, and other buildings in Gila Bend were destroyed. People were left homeless. They lost almost everything they owned. They were desperately in need of shelter, medical care, and assistance in rebuilding their community or in moving elsewhere. They did not have enough money to pay for the things they needed, so they asked the state government to use tax funds to help them.

What do *you* think?

1. Does the principle of similarity justify denying Gila Bend's request for extra tax money?

2. What might be some consequences of denying Gila Bend's request?

3. Which consequences would be advantages? Which would be disadvantages?

4. What should be done? Why?

5. What are the values and interests that you considered in reaching your decision?

Critical Thinking Exercise
EXAMINING COMMON DIFFICULTIES IN APPLYING THE PRINCIPLE OF SIMILARITY

Giving grades to students is a situation in which issues of distributive justice commonly arise. This exercise illustrates two of the most common difficulties in using the principle of similarity:

1. People may disagree about which similarities or differences among people should be considered in a particular situation.

2. People may disagree about what degree of similarity or difference justifies treating people alike or differently.

Working in small groups, read the following situations and answer the questions which follow. Be prepared to discuss your answers with the class.

1. Suppose a student in an English class has received C+ grades throughout the semester on all assignments, tests, and class participation. The student is in the senior year of high school, and **needs** a B in the course to get into college. Should the student's need be considered in addition to his desert in giving the grade? Should any other considerations, such as effort, be used?

2. Now suppose the student claims that his scores on all assignments, tests, and class performance are not different enough from the students getting a B- grade to justify treating him differently by giving him a C+ grade. How can you evaluate the student's claim?

What do *you* think?

1. Should desert be the only idea used in deciding a fair distribution of grades or awards? Should need or capacity be considered also?

2. What difficulties might arise from trying to decide which idea—need, capacity, or desert—should be given most consideration in making a decision involving a particular issue of distributive justice?

3. What kinds of difficulties might arise from trying to decide if persons or groups are similar or different in regard to their needs, capacities, or desert? What examples of such difficulties can you give from your experiences?

Using the Lesson

1. Before 1920, the laws of most states did not allow women to vote. Do you think these laws were based mainly on ideas of need, capacity, or desert?

   Since 1920, women have been guaranteed the right to vote by the Nineteenth Amendment to the U.S. Constitution. Do you think this provision of the Constitution is based mainly on ideas of need, capacity or desert? Explain you answers.

2. Describe a situation in which someone made a decision about distributive justice that you think was wrong. Explain why you think the decision was wrong, and what you think the right decision would have been. Explain the considerations you used in reaching your position.

LESSON 4

Who Should Get the Job?

Purpose of Lesson

This lesson gives you the opportunity to use intellectual tools to decide who should receive the benefit of employment. You will examine an imaginary situation in which a newly elected mayor must choose one candidate for a position. Then you will be asked to give your opinion on the issue and defend it.

When you have completed this lesson, you should be able to explain how you have used the intellectual tools you have learned in evaluating, taking, and defending positions on the issue of distributive justice.

Critical Thinking Exercise
SELECTING SOMEONE FOR A POSITION

In this exercise your class will role-play the selection of a Special Advisor on Community Relations. Your class will be divided into five groups. One group will be the mayor's employment panel, which makes recommendations to the mayor regarding employment decisions. The other four groups will represent the four applicants for the position of Special Advisor on Community Relations. All groups should read the following situation and complete the chart on page 188.

Each of the groups representing the four candidates should develop arguments to persuade the mayor's employment panel to recommend that group's candidate. The fifth group will be the mayor's employment panel. It will hear each group's presentation. Then it will decide who to recommend to the mayor. The mayor's employment panel should develop questions to ask members of the other groups. After hearing the groups' presentations and asking questions, the mayor's employment panel should discuss the candidates and decide who to recommend for the position. Finally, the panel should explain the reasons for its decision to the class.

What arguments can you make to support your group's candidate?

Who Should Be Selected as Special Advisor?

Alicia Olsen ran for mayor of Parkside and won. Parkside is a city of about 100,000 people. The community includes several ethnic and racial groups which have had some conflict in the past.

The mayor appointed a group of people as an employment panel to advise her on employment decisions. She was particularly concerned to get the panel's advice on filling the position of Special Advisor on Community Relations. The person given this job would be responsible for

- meeting with community groups to hear their concerns

- keeping the mayor informed about neighborhood problems

- recommending solutions to those problems

- carrying out programs to improve relations among different ethnic and racial groups in the community

A number of people made recommendations to the mayor about filling the position.

Alicia's campaign manager suggested the job should be given to someone who contributed time, effort, and money to Alicia's campaign for mayor. He said that loyal supporters should be rewarded for their efforts. Giving the job to a campaign supporter would be a good way to show her appreciation for the assistance she had been given. The personnel manager of the City of Parkside suggested the job should be given to someone with experience working with community groups, who had a record of successfully fulfilling the kinds of responsibilities the job required.

The president of a minority rights group reminded the mayor that prejudice had prevented members of minority groups from having a fair chance to work in key positions in Parkside government. He suggested that the job be given to a candidate who was a member of a minority group so that the interests of minorities would be represented. This would help make up for past discrimination against minority groups in city government.

Alicia finally narrowed the field to four finalists for the employment panel to evaluate.

Bill Spangler was a newcomer to Parkside. For the past five years he had been a community affairs specialist in a neighboring town. In that job, Bill had developed citizen involvement programs, a "hot line" to the city hall for citizen complaints, and a program to train members of various ethnic and minority groups to fill positions in city government. He had a college degree in city management.

Kim Villas had been active for a long time attempting to secure equal rights for minorities. She had received the Parkside Citizen of the Year award for her efforts. She also was one of the most active workers in the campaign to elect Alicia.

Charles Daly was one of Alicia's strongest supporters and fund-raisers. He had supported her not only in her race for mayor, but also in other campaigns when she had run successfully for city council. Although Daly had little experience in community relations, he formerly managed the City Park Department. While doing so, he developed several successful community recreation programs.

Dotty Vickers was one of Alicia's oldest friends and supporters. At one time, Dotty contributed $5,000 to Alicia's campaign for city council. Since then, she had lost most of her money and she was very much in need of a job. She had 20 years of experience as a social worker in a large, nearby city before moving to Parkside.

Using the Lesson

1. Write a letter to Mayor Olsen stating who you would select for the job. Explain the reasons for your decision.

2. Interview adults who are responsible for hiring decisions. Ask them to describe the considerations they use in choosing among candidates. Compare their ideas with those you have just studied.

3. Working with your teacher, invite an elected official to class to describe considerations used in selecting persons to work in his or her office.

Intellectual Tool Chart for Issues of Distributive Justice	
Questions	Answers
1. What benefit or burden is to be distributed?	
2. Who are the persons being considered to receive the benefit or burden?	
3. What important similarities or differences are there among the persons in terms of a. **need** b. **capacity** c. **desert**	
4. Which of the similarities and differences listed above should be taken into account in deciding who should receive the benefit or burden? Explain your position.	
5. Based on the similarities and differences you have decided to take into account, what would be a **fair** way to distribute the benefit or burden?	
6. What might be the **advantages** and **disadvantages** of doing what is fair? Would **other values** and **interests** be served by a different distribution of the benefit or burden?	
7. How do you think the benefit or burden should be distributed? Explain your position.	

LESSON 5

How Would You Select Students to Participate in a Music Program?

Purpose of Lesson

This lesson provides the opportunity to use what you have learned to evaluate a plan for the selection of students to participate in a music program. Your class will role-play a school board hearing at which the plan is discussed. When you have completed the lesson, you should be able to evaluate, take, and defend positions on the fairness of the plan.

Critical Thinking Exercise
EVALUATING THE FAIRNESS OF A PLAN

Read the following situation. Then, working in small groups, complete the chart on page 192. Be prepared to take and justify a position on what policy should be used to distribute the benefit of special music classes among students.

The Music Program

The Farmington School District had not provided a music program in its high schools for a number of years. The school district did not have funds available to hire music teachers or to buy musical instruments. Students who wanted to receive music training had to pay for private lessons and buy their own instruments. The families of some students had enough money to pay for their children's music education, but many did not.

Recently, the school district received money from the State Department of Education to provide a music education program for the next five years. The funds were not sufficient, however, for the district to provide music education for all students. The school district had to decide which students would be eligible for the special music education classes and which students would not be eligible.

What do you think would be a fair way to select students for music education classes?

The school board asked the superintendent to develop a fair plan. After consulting with teachers, and interested parents' groups, the superintendent developed the following plan to present to the school board for its approval.

The Plan

1. The high school will hold try-outs for students interested in enrolling in the new music education program. Students participating in the try-outs will be judged on the basis of their skill in singing or playing a musical instrument.

2. Seventy-five percent of the places in the program will be filled by those who demonstrate the most musical knowledge and skill.

3. Twenty-five percent of the places in the program will be filled by a random drawing. All students who are not selected during the try-outs will have their names placed in a large container, and names will be drawn until the remaining places in the program are filled.

Critical Thinking Exercise
ROLE-PLAYING A SCHOOL BOARD HEARING

Your class will complete this exercise by role playing a school board hearing on the proposed plan.

Preparing for the Hearing

The class should be divided into the following groups:

1. **School Superintendent and staff**
   You prepared the plan that has been presented to the school board.

2. **Students and Parents for Equality**
   You want to ensure fair and equal educational opportunities for all students.

3. **Music Appreciation Society**
   You want to promote the appreciation of good music and to create opportunities for the best possible music to be performed in your community.

4. **Farmington School Board**
   You must decide how the limited music education opportunities will be distributed among the students in the school district.

The first group should prepare arguments to support the proposed plan.

The next two groups should develop their own positions on the plan and, if they wish, prepare alternate plans to suggest to the school board.

Each group should select two or three spokespersons to present its position to the school board. While these groups are developing their positions, the school board members should prepare to ask questions and should select a chairperson to conduct the hearing.

Conducting the Hearing

Each group should present its position or plan to the school board. During group presentations, board members may ask questions. After all groups have made their presentations, the board should discuss the proposals and decide how opportunities to participate in the music education program will be distributed. The board members should explain the reasons for their decision to the class.

Using the Lesson

1. Which ideas (need, capacity, desert) would you consider in selecting students for

   ■ the school soccer team
   ■ advanced math class
   ■ special tutoring
   ■ student government

   Besides fairness, what other values and interests would you consider? Explain your reasoning.

2. Ask a school administrator to visit the class and explain school policies on the distribution of special educational opportunities. Discuss how the ideas of need, capacity, and desert are used in the policies.

3. Ask your teacher, a librarian, or an attorney to help you find a written account of the Supreme Court's decision in *Fullilove v. Klutznick*, 448 U.S. 448 (1980), or of another court case dealing with an issue of distributive justice. Read the facts in the case and the decision of the court, and summarize them for class discussion.

Intellectual Tool Chart for Issues of Distributive Justice

Questions	Answers
1. What benefit or burden is to be distributed?	
2. Who are the persons being considered to receive the benefit or burden?	
3. What important similarities or differences are there among the persons in terms of a. **need** b. **capacity** c. **desert**	
4. Which of the similarities and differences listed above should be taken into account in deciding who should receive the benefit or burden? Explain your position.	
5. Based on the similarities and differences you have decided to take into account, what would be a **fair** way to distribute the benefit or burden?	
6. What might be the **advantages** and **disadvantages** of doing what is fair? Would **other values** and **interests** be served by a different distribution of the benefit or burden?	
7. How do you think the benefit or burden should be distributed? Explain your position.	

Unit Three: What Is Corrective Justice?

How do the situations illustrated in these pictures raise issues of corrective justice?

Purpose of Unit

This unit deals with **corrective justice**, that is, with issues of **fair** or **proper responses** to wrongs and injuries. In this unit, you will learn the goals of corrective justice. You also will learn a new set of intellectual tools that are useful in evaluating, taking, and defending positions on issues of corrective justice.

When you have completed this unit, you should be able to define corrective justice and explain its goals. You also should be able to use the intellectual tools to evaluate issues of corrective justice and make thoughtful decisions about how to respond to wrongs and injuries.

LESSON 6

What Are the Goals of Corrective Justice?

Purpose of Lesson
This lesson explains the idea of corrective justice and introduces you to the goals of corrective justice. When you have completed the lesson, you should be able to define corrective justice and explain its goals.

Terms to Know

correction
prevention
deterrence

Critical Thinking Exercise
EXAMINING ISSUES OF CORRECTIVE JUSTICE

Corrective justice refers to the fairness of responses to wrongs or injuries. Each of the following situations involves an issue of corrective justice.

Work in small groups to read the situations and answer the questions that follow them. Be prepared to explain your answers to the class.

- Katherine's mother's car was hit by a truck driver. Both Katherine and her mother were hurt and had to be hospitalized. Their medical bills amounted to over $10,000. Because the truck driver was responsible for the accident, he had to pay for their medical bills and car repairs.

- Just before an election for mayor in a small town, a local newspaper opposed to one of the candidates printed several stories which hinted that the candidate might be guilty of taking bribes and having connections with organized crime.

The candidate lost the election and sued the newspaper. During the trial the staff members of the newspaper could not present any evidence to back their stories or show they had carefully investigated the stories before printing them. The candidate presented evidence to support his position that, if it had not been for the articles, he would have won the election. The court ordered the newspaper to pay the campaign costs of the candidate and an additional $20,000 in damages.

- Two men were arrested and convicted of selling narcotics to teenagers. They were then sentenced to prison terms of three to five years.

What do *you* think?

1. Explain what you think is fair or unfair about each of the above responses to wrongs or injuries.

2. Explain what values and interests might be important to think about when deciding

what would be a proper response to a wrong or injury.

What is the need for corrective justice?

Wherever there are people living together in groups, situations will arise in which people commit wrongs or cause injuries to others. **Corrective justice** is concerned with **fair or proper responses to wrongs or injuries.**

Responses to wrongs or injuries may vary widely. Sometimes it may be enough merely to **inform** someone that he or she has wronged or injured another. At other times we may require someone to take the responsibility of setting things right by **paying** for the wrong or injury. And under some circumstances we may **punish** a person in one way or another for committing a wrong or causing an injury. These and other common responses to wrongs and injuries will be discussed in detail in a later lesson. First, however, we will examine the goals or purposes of corrective justice.

What are the goals of corrective justice?

When someone has committed a wrong, or has caused an injury to another by wrongful conduct, we usually want to correct the situation—to "set things right." Additionally, we may want to prevent or discourage future wrongful conduct by "teaching a lesson" to the wrongdoer or by "making an example" of him or her. Thus, the purposes or goals of corrective justice are

- **correction**—providing a remedy or imposing a penalty to set things right in a **fair** way

- **prevention**—responding to wrongdoing in a way that will prevent the person from doing wrong again

- **deterrence**—discouraging people from committing wrongs and causing injuries, for fear of the consequences

---

Using the Lesson

1. Work with a study partner or in small groups. Make a list of the most common responses to wrongs or injuries that you have observed.

2. What are some situations of which you are aware in which a response to a wrong or injury has been fair? Why was it fair?

3. What are some situations you are aware of in which a response to a wrong or injury was unfair? Why was it unfair?

4. What might happen in a family, school, community, or nation if no attempts were made to provide fair responses to wrongs or injuries among people? Why?

LESSON 7

What Intellectual Tools Are Useful in Making Decisions About Issues of Corrective Justice?

Purpose of Lesson

This lesson introduces you to some intellectual tools which are useful in resolving issues of corrective justice. When you have completed this lesson, you should be able to explain and use these intellectual tools. Other intellectual tools which you can use to evaluate, take, and defend positions on issues of corrective justice will be introduced in the next lesson.

Terms to Know

wrong
injury
extent
duration
impact
offensiveness
intent
recklessness
carelessness
regret

How can we decide upon fair or proper responses to wrongs and injuries?

As you have learned, a basic goal of corrective justice is to "set things right" in a fair way when a wrong or injury has happened. Other important goals of corrective justice are to prevent additional wrongs or injuries and to deter others from committing such wrongs or injuries.

Deciding what is fair may be simple in some situations, such as when a young child takes away the toy (property) of another child. Our sense of justice may be met by merely restoring the toy.

Our interest in preventing such things from happening again may be met by informing the child that it is wrong to take another person's property without permission. It is hoped these actions will teach the child proper behavior.

In other situations, finding a fair response to a wrong or injury may be more difficult. Unfortunately, there is no simple formula for deciding what would be proper responses in difficult situations. However, there are a number of intellectual tools that can be useful when making such decisions.

Following are some of these intellectual tools. They form the first three steps of a procedure you can use to examine situations in which a wrong or injury has happened. Simple examples have been added to each step in the procedure to illustrate its usefulness. In the lessons that follow, you will learn the intellectual tools you need to complete the remaining steps of the procedure. You will be asked to apply this procedure and use these intellectual tools to examine and take positions on some interesting problems of corrective justice.

Critical Thinking Exercise
EXAMINING INTELLECTUAL TOOLS

This exercise may best be accomplished during a class discussion, or you may wish to examine the steps in small groups and then discuss your responses with the entire class.

Read each step below and the questions and examples that it includes. Then be prepared to

- discuss the usefulness of each step

- give examples of its application from your own experiences and observations

Step 1. Identify the important characteristics of the wrong or injury.

a. What was the wrong or injury?

-   A **wrong** is conduct that violates a duty or responsibility imposed by laws, rules, customs, or moral principles.
-   An **injury** is harm or damage to persons or property, or violation of a person's rights.

In some cases, conduct may be wrong and also cause an injury. In other cases, conduct may be wrong but not cause an injury. And in some cases there may be injuries without wrongful conduct.

For example: Look at each of the following situations and answer the question: Was there a WRONG, an INJURY, or both?

(1) George drove his car through a red light but no accident resulted.

(2) Monica did not fix the car properly before she rented it to a customer. The car's left front wheel fell off while the customer was driving, and she was injured when the car skidded off the road and hit a parked truck.

(3) Paul and Maggie were playing baseball. Maggie threw a ball that hit Paul in the shoulder. For the next few days Paul's shoulder hurt.

b. How **serious** was the wrong or injury?

In order to decide how serious a wrong or injury may be, it is often helpful to look for the answers to four questions. The following situations are designed to illustrate the usefulness of each of these questions.

Suppose it was discovered that tuna, an important game and food fish, were about to become extinct because of overfishing. To protect the fish, the government passed a law limiting the amount of tuna that might be caught by any one company to 500 per day. Two fishing companies broke the law and caught more than 500 per day. To determine how serious the wrong or injury may be, it is often helpful to look at a situation and answer the following four questions:

(1) What was the **extent** of the wrong or injury?

Over a six-day period the Tuna Can Company caught 6,000 tuna, or 3,000 over what they were allowed.

The Albacore Company caught 3,050 tuna over the same six-day period, or 50 over what they were allowed.

(2) What was the **duration** of the wrong or injury?

The Tuna Can Company broke the law for six days before being caught.

The Albacore Company only broke the law for one day.

(3) What was the **impact** of the wrong or injury?

The Tuna Can Company caught 1,000 tuna fish in one day.

The Albacore Company caught 550 in one day.

(4) How **offensive** was the wrong or injury?

The owners of the Tuna Can Company were aware of what they were doing and had intended to catch as many tuna as they could in order to benefit by the higher prices being paid for the scarce tuna.

The owners of the Albacore Company had tried to stay within the limit but were careless in counting the tuna they had caught.

Step 2. Identify the important characteristics of the person or persons causing the wrong or injury.

The following are five questions that should be answered about the person or persons causing a wrong or injury before deciding what to do.

a. What was the person's **state of mind** at the time he or she caused the wrong or injury?

A person's state of mind is one of the most important things to consider when trying to find a fair response to a wrong or injury. To determine the person's state of mind, a number of things should be considered. They are

(1) **Intent:** Did the person act intentionally (on purpose) to bring about the wrong or injury?

(2) **Recklessness:** Did the person deliberately (or knowingly) ignore obvious risks of serious harm?

(3) **Carelessness:** Did the person act in a thoughtless manner, without paying enough attention to risks that were foreseeable?

(4) **Knowledge of Probable Consequences:** Did the person know, or have the capability of knowing, that what he or she was doing was wrong or likely to cause an injury?

(5) **Control:** Did the person have physical and mental control over his or her actions?

(6) **Duty or Obligation:** Did the person have a duty to act, or not act, in a certain way in order to prevent the wrong or injury?

(7) **More Important Values and Interests:** Did the person have any other important values, interests, responsibilities, or motives that might justify or excuse his or her actions?

The following imaginary situation is designed to illustrate the usefulness of the ideas described in this section on **state of mind**.

Xavier Kahn, the commander of a space ship from a planet at war with other planets, was accused of destroying the crops and shelter of a neutral space station, leaving its inhabitants without food and shelter.

The following facts were revealed at his trial. Examine these facts to find out what Xavier Kahn's **state of mind** was when he caused the wrongs and injuries to the neutral space station.

■ Xavier Kahn and his troopers herded everyone in the space station. He informed them he was going to destroy their crops in order to prevent the food from falling into enemy hands, even though the station was neutral.

- Xavier Kahn thought he could limit the fire's destruction to the crops, but he was wrong. The fire spread and destroyed most of the buildings on the station, leaving the inhabitants without food or shelter. However, Kahn left them with temporary shelters and enough food for about a week by which time he thought help would come from the nation that owned the station.

- At his trial, one of Kahn's officers testified that by the time they had reached the station, their space ship was badly damaged, they were out of food, crew members were ill and injured, Kahn hadn't slept for days and his "ship was in trouble," and he had just been informed that his brother had been killed in a training accident.

b. What was the person's **past history**? Has the person committed similar wrongs or caused similar injuries in the past?

Suppose that Xavier Kahn had an excellent record as an officer and a history of respect for human rights. Should his excellent record be considered in deciding what should be done in response to his wrongdoing?

c. What **character and personality traits** has the person shown? Is the person generally trustworthy, careful, considerate of another's rights, and nonviolent?

Suppose that one of Kahn's officers testified that Kahn flew into rages over little things, that most of his men feared him, and that he had a deep hatred for the nation that owned the space station in spite of its neutrality?

d. What **feelings** did the person express? Does the person **regret** (feel sorry about) his or her conduct, or is the person unconcerned about the wrong or injury he or she caused?

At his trial, Kahn testified that, "There were wrongs committed—wrongs for which I as commander am responsible." It was clear from his testimony that Kahn was sorry for his actions.

e. What was the person's **role** in causing the wrong or injury? Did the person act alone or with others, as a leader or minor participant?

During his testimony, Kahn took sole responsibility for his actions. However, other officers testified that before landing on the space station, all of the officers of the ship had met with Kahn and agreed they should destroy the crops of the neutral station to prevent them falling into enemy hands.

Step 3. Identify the important characteristics of the person or persons who were wronged or injured.

Besides looking at the relevant characteristics of the person or persons causing the wrong or injury, there may be important characteristics about the person or persons who suffered the wrong or injury that should be considered. The following two questions are designed to focus your attention on this "side of the coin."

a. Did the person or persons **contribute** to causing the wrong or injury?

Suppose when Xavier Kahn landed on the space station he had asked for food for his hungry men and had been refused. Furthermore, the people living on the station had attacked them and tried to destroy their space ship. Could it be said that the people

on the station contributed to the wrongs or injuries they suffered?

b. What is the person's **ability to recover** from the wrong or injury?

Suppose that because of radiation from the weapons used by Kahn's men, it will not be possible to grow crops on station land for five years. If the crops had been destroyed by less drastic measures the land could have grown another crop within a few months. Should this be taken into consideration when deciding what response should be made?

What do *you* think?

1. Are the steps listed above enough to consider when deciding how to correct a wrong or injury? What other considerations should be added?

2. What should be the purposes of correcting wrongs and injuries?

Using the Lesson

1. Bring to class excerpts from newspapers or descriptions of television news or entertainment programs, in which issues of corrective justice are raised. Determine and explain which of the tools you have studied were used in making decisions about how to respond to the wrongs and injuries in the situations.

2. Working with your teacher, invite a judge or attorney to class to discuss how the intellectual tools you have studied in this lesson are used in court cases.

LESSON 8

What Responses Can We Make to Wrongs and Injuries?

Purpose of Lesson

This lesson introduces you to the remaining two steps to use in dealing with issues of corrective justice and provides a chart listing all the steps and considerations. You will apply the procedure to take a position on how to respond to a situation in which a wrong and injury have occurred. When you have completed the lesson, you should be able to use the intellectual tools you have learned to examine and take positions on issues of corrective justice.

Terms to Know

deter
inform
pardon
avenge
restore
compensate
human dignity
proportionality

What are the five steps to use in examining issues of corrective justice?

So far, you have considered the first three steps in the procedure to be used in deciding issues of corrective justice: (1) identifying important characteristics of the wrong or injury, (2) identifying important characteristics of the person or persons causing the wrong or injury, and (3) identifying important characteristics of the person or persons wronged or injured. Two steps remain in this procedure: (4) examining common responses to wrongs and injuries and their

purposes, and (5) considering related values and interests to decide what would be the best response.

Critical Thinking Exercise
EXAMINING INTELLECTUAL TOOLS

After you have read the following two steps remaining in the procedure, be prepared to

- discuss the usefulness of each step

- give examples of their application to situations you have experienced or observed

Step 4. Examine common responses to wrongs and injuries and their purposes.

As mentioned earlier, the principal goal of corrective justice is to provide a fair or proper response to a wrong or injury, to "set things right." Responses may be used not only to **correct** wrongs or injuries, but also to **prevent** those responsible from causing further wrongs or injuries, and to **deter** or discourage others from causing wrongs or injuries. Following is a list of common responses to wrongs and injuries and a brief explanation of the purposes of each. Often more than one of the responses listed may be chosen, and often more than one purpose may be involved.

a. We may **inform** or tell the wrongdoer that what he or she did was wrong or caused injury.

For example:

(1) Doug and Jack were water-skiing. While Doug was pulling Jack on the skis, their boat was stopped by a park ranger. She told them they could not ski without another person on board the boat to

Purpose: The purpose of this type of response is to prevent future wrongs and injuries by explaining to the wrongdoer how his or her conduct was wrong or caused injury. In these cases, the wrong or injury goes uncorrected.

b. We may **overlook** or **ignore** a wrong or injury.

For example:

(1) When the J-M Company truck was delivering a new television set to Kevin's house, the driver accidentally ran over Kevin's prize rose bush. Although Kevin was upset, he chose to do nothing about it.

watch the skier. The law requires this because the person driving the boat needs to watch where he or she is going, and cannot keep the skier in view at the same time. Doug and Jack promised they would obey the law in the future, so the park ranger decided not to fine them.

(2) Recently, one city changed its posted maximum speed limit signs to read in kilometers instead of miles per hour. Many residents were confused by the change. When John was stopped by a police officer for exceeding the posted speed limit, he explained to the officer that his automobile registered his speed in miles per hour. The officer patiently informed John that the kilometers were also listed on his speedometer in blue numbers. Then she allowed John to proceed without giving him a ticket for speeding.

(2) Mrs. Johnson was a nursery-school teacher. One of her younger students repeatedly clapped his hands while she was attempting to read a story to the class. Mrs. Johnson generally ignored his behavior.

Purpose: Sometimes we decide to overlook or ignore a wrong or injury because it is not worth the time and effort to try to correct it. Sometimes we may believe the wrongdoer is just trying to get some attention. Ignoring the wrongful act may deter such conduct in the future. In these cases the wrong or injury goes uncorrected.

c. We may **forgive** or **pardon** the wrongdoer for a wrong or injury.

For example:

(1) Carrie promised her mother that she would lock the house before leaving for school. Carrie forgot to do so, and someone went inside and stole their TV and stereo equipment. Carrie was extremely upset; so was her mother. Carrie's mother forgave her for her mistake, however, knowing that she had learned a valuable lesson about carrying out her responsibilities.

(2) Sue loaned $1,000 to her friend, Mike. Mike agreed to repay Sue over a period of one year. Mike lost his job and was unable to repay the loan. Instead of pursuing the matter in court, Sue decided not to make Mike repay her.

Purpose: Sometimes we decide to forgive or pardon wrongful acts in the hope that this will cause the wrongdoers to regret their actions and "mend their ways." Sometimes we decide to forgive or pardon a wrongdoer out of the belief that he or she has already suffered enough. In these cases the wrong or injury goes uncorrected.

d. We may **punish** the wrongdoer for a wrong or injury.

For example:

(1) Convicted of burglarizing two homes, Sylvia, aged 18, Marie, aged 20, and Sam, aged 20, were sentenced to six months in jail.

(2) When Martin's mother discovered he had skipped school, she made him stay in his room all weekend, refused to let him watch television, and made him promise never to skip school again.

Purpose: One purpose of punishment is corrective justice, that is, to **avenge** or "get even" for a wrong or injury. Punishment also may prevent future wrongs and injuries by "teaching the person a lesson." It also may deter others from wrongdoing by "setting an example."

e. We may require the wrongdoer to **restore** or give back something he or she has taken.

For example:

After returning from the supermarket, Mrs. Tong noticed her five-year-old son playing with a toy fire engine. Mrs. Tong asked her son where he got the fire engine. He told her he had taken it from the store. Realizing that the fire engine had not been paid for, Mrs. Tong promptly took her son and the fire engine back to the store and asked to speak to the store manager. In front of her son, Mrs. Tong explained what had happened and had the boy personally hand back the toy.

Purpose: When a wrongdoer has taken things that can be returned to their owner, we may require the wrongdoer to restore or give back the items in order to "set things right." Requiring a wrongdoer to restore what he or she has taken also may serve to prevent or deter future wrongs and injuries.

f. We may require the wrongdoer to **compensate** or pay for a wrong or injury.

For example:

(1) After borrowing a book from the library, Mr. Burns lost it. He had to pay the price of a new book to compensate for the one he had lost.

(2) An automobile manufacturer was sued for damages when one of its cars exploded, killing the driver. After a trial, the jury awarded $1,000,000 to the driver's wife to compensate for the loss of her husband. The court made the manufacturer pay this amount to the driver's wife.

Purpose: In many cases a wrong or injury cannot be "undone" in the sense that the items taken, damaged or destroyed cannot be restored or put back. In such cases, we may require the wrongdoer to compensate for the loss by paying money or giving something of value to the wronged or injured person. Requiring a wrongdoer to compensate or pay for a wrong or injury also may serve to prevent or deter future wrongs and injuries.

g. We may provide **treatment** or **education** to the wrongdoer.

For example:

(1) Carlo was driving too fast and got a ticket for speeding. Because it was his first offense, he was permitted to attend driving school instead of paying a fine.

(2) In Topeka, Kansas, all persons sentenced to prison receive tests and treatment from psychiatrists and other mental health experts. Studies show that these prisoners are 25% less likely to return to prison after release than prisoners who do not receive treatment.

Purpose: Providing treatment or education to wrongdoers is not intended to correct the wrong or injury they caused. Its purpose is to prevent them from causing further wrongs or injuries by giving them the knowledge and skills to become responsible members of society.

Step 5. Consider other values and interests in determining a response.

When we try to decide what response to make to a wrong or injury, we need to consider what values and interests may be promoted or undermined by a particular response.

a. What responses would **correct** the wrong or injury?

Our need for corrective justice might be satisfied by responses that "set things right" in one way or another, such as those that require a person to give back something taken from another person, compensate a person for a loss, or those that place a burden or punishment on a wrongdoer.

However, it is important to remember that a response may be chosen to serve other values and interests, rather than to serve the goals of corrective justice. For example, if a friend were to break something of yours by accident, you might not ask or allow her to replace it or pay for it.

b. How might a response **deter** or **prevent** future wrongs or injuries?

In many situations, one of the main reasons for selecting a particular response to a wrong or injury is that the response probably will prevent the wrongdoer from committing such actions in the future and will deter other people from committing such actions.

For example, sending someone who has committed a crime to prison removes the person from society. It is hoped that when the person is released, he or she will refrain from such actions in the future. Others, who value their freedom, may be deterred from wrongdoing because they do not wish to be imprisoned.

c. How might a response affect **distributive justice?**

Distributive justice requires that "like cases be treated alike." Cases that are different in important ways should be treated differently.

For example, suppose two persons with similar backgrounds and criminal records are caught stealing. Both are tried and convicted. If one of the persons was sentenced to prison and the other was placed on probation, the response might be considered a violation of distributive justice.

d. How might a response affect **human dignity**?

An important belief held by many people is that all persons, no matter what their actions, should be treated with **dignity**—as persons of value with basic rights, deserving respect as human beings. For example, responses that are cruel should not be used no matter how offensive a person's crime may be.

e. How might a response affect **preservation of human life**?

Many believe that human life has a basic worth or value and should be protected. Some people say that the death penalty conflicts with this value, even when it is imposed for taking the life of another person. Others argue that the death penalty deters potential murderers, and that it promotes the value of human life.

f. What responses are **practical** given the resources available?

Individuals and society (the public) need to make efficient use of their time, energy, and property when making responses to wrongs and injuries. The costs of various responses must be considered and, in some instances, a response which sets things completely right may prove too costly.

For example, under our system, society pays for the costs of gathering evidence against criminal wrongdoers, trying them in a court, and, if they are found guilty, sometimes placing them in a prison or other institution. However, society usually does not pay the victim for any losses he or she may have suffered as a result of criminal wrongdoing.

g. How might a response affect **freedom**? To what extent can limitations on the freedom of the wrongdoer be justified?

Our society, like many others, places a high value on individual liberty, choice, movement, and expression. In selecting a

Why should we consider principles of distributive justice in deciding on responses to wrongs and injuries?

response, the value of the freedom of the wrongdoer as well as all members of society should be considered.

h. How might a response affect **proportionality?**

A fundamental consideration in judging whether a response is fair is whether it is in proportion to the seriousness of the wrong or injury. For example, the response to a cold-blooded murder should be more serious than the response to stealing a bicycle. This is what we mean when we say "the punishment should fit the crime."

i. How might a response satisfy the desire for **revenge?**

Since ancient times, humans have included in their ideas of justice the desire for revenge. Today some people believe revenge should not be a consideration in selecting or evaluating responses. Others, however, feel the desire for revenge is natural and can be considered in allowing society to "get even" as a part of setting things right.

NOTE: Sometimes there may be a conflict between the foregoing values and interests. For instance, society places a high value upon the protection of its citizens from crimes. On the other hand, society places a high value upon the freedom of the individual. The following examples demonstrate these conflicting values.

- One state had a law which prohibited children under the age of 12 from selling newspapers or magazines in any street or public place. A woman and her nine-year-old daughter, residents of that state, sold religious pamphlets for five cents each on a busy street corner. The woman was arrested and convicted for violating the state's child labor law. She appealed on the basis that the law was a violation of her right to exercise her religious freedom.

- Should a wrongdoer who does not present a current threat to the freedom or wellbeing of other members of society be deprived of his or her freedom or should some other response be made to the wrongdoing?

What do *you* think?

1. After reviewing the section on common responses to wrongs and injuries, how would you answer the following questions?

   a. If an adult has committed a wrong in the past and he or she has been told about it, what should be the response if it happens again? Would your answer be different if the wrongdoer were a juvenile?

   b. How serious must the wrong or injury be that overlooking or ignoring it will not satisfy our sense of corrective justice?

   c. Can forgiving or pardoning a wrongdoer offend our sense of distributive justice if it means that some would then suffer more than others? If not, why not?

2. What is the purpose of considering the values and interests that may be promoted or undermined by various responses to a wrong or injury?

3. How might the considerations noted above help insure the fairness with which wrongs and injuries are corrected?

Critical Thinking Exercise
TAKING POSITIONS ON AN ISSUE
OF CORRECTIVE JUSTICE

The class should be divided into small groups. Each group should read the following selection and then complete the chart on pages 209–210. Use the chart to develop a position on the response that was made to the wrongs and injuries described in the selection.

The Accident

Glen Duncan was taking his friend, Wendy Phillips, for a ride in his brand new sports car. Suddenly a Chevy crossed over from the other lane and hit Glen's car head-on. Glen's new car was demolished. He received a minor concussion and Wendy suffered two broken ribs.

The Chevy was driven by Karen Adams. Karen was an alcoholic. She was not injured in the accident, but she was incoherent and her breath reeked of alcohol.

When officers on the scene asked her to walk in a straight line, she had trouble maintaining her balance. Her speech was slurred. A sample of her blood was taken. It showed that Karen had a blood alcohol content of .20 percent. A person with such a high blood alcohol content is considered in many states to be under the influence of alcohol and unable to operate a car safely.

At her trial, Karen testified that she had taken three drinks before getting into her car. She also said she did not remember anything about the accident.

Karen did not argue with any of the evidence introduced at the trial. Instead, she presented an argument which challenged the idea of punishing alcoholics, such as herself, through the criminal justice system. She argued that alcoholics are sick and should be helped with medical treatment rather than punished.

How would you respond to the wrongs and injuries described in this story?

The prosecutor, on the other hand, argued that innocent people must be protected from drunk drivers. The prosecutor said that the best way to insure protection was to take drunk drivers off the streets and put them behind bars.

Karen was convicted by a jury of having caused a serious injury while driving under the influence of alcohol. She was sentenced to spend 60 days in jail.

What do *you* think?

1. What would be the best response(s) to the wrongs and injuries described in the story?

2. Are the responses you suggested designed to correct the wrongs or injuries?

3. Are the responses you suggested designed to prevent further wrongs or injuries?

Using the Lesson

1. Interview people responsible for dealing with wrongs and injuries as a part of their profession. Such persons might include police officers, lawyers, judges, probation officers, or school principals. Ask the persons to describe some of the situations they have had to deal with and what ideas they have used in making decisions on the best responses to wrongs and injuries.

2. Do research to find out how different societies respond to one of the following crimes:

   - murder
   - robbery
   - theft of government property

   Present a report to the class describing what you learn.

3. Draw a cartoon to illustrate a situation involving an issue of corrective justice, specifically showing one or more of the intellectual tools you have studied in this lesson.

Intellectual Tool Chart for Issues of Corrective Justice

Questions	Answers

1. **Identify the wrong or injury:**
a. What was the wrong, if any?
 	
b. What was the injury, if any?
 	
c. How serious was the wrong or injury? Consider:
   (1) extent
   (2) duration
   (3) impact
   (4) offensiveness	

2. **Identify important characteristics of the person causing the wrong or injury:**
a. What was the person's **state of mind**? Consider:
   (1) intent
   (2) recklessness
   (3) carelessness
   (4) knowledge of probable consequences
   (5) control or choice
   (6) duty or obligation
   (7) important values, interests, or responsibilities
 	
b. What facts about the person's **past history** are relevant in deciding upon a fair response?
 	
c. What facts about the person's **character** are relevant in deciding upon a fair response?
 	
d. What **feelings** did the person express after causing the wrong or injury?
 	
e. What was the person's **role** in causing the wrong or injury?	

3. **Identify important characteristics of the person wronged or injured:** a. Did the person **contribute** to causing the wrong or injury he or she suffered? b. Will the person be able to **recover** from the wrong or injury?	

Intellectual Tool Chart for Issues of Corrective Justice	
Questions	**Answers**
4. **Examine common responses to wrongs and injuries and their purposes**: a. Should we **inform** the person that what he or she did was wrong or injurious? Why? b. Should we **overlook** or **ignore** the wrong or injury? Why? c. Should we **forgive** or **pardon** the person for causing the wrong or injury? Why? d. Should we **punish** the person for causing the wrong or injury? Why? e. Should we require the person to **restore** what was taken or damaged? Why? f. Should we require the person to **compensate** for causing the wrong or injury? Why? g. Should we provide **treatment** or **education**? Why?	
5. **Consider related values and interests**: a. What responses would **correct** the wrong or injury? b. What responses would **deter** or **prevent** future wrongs or injuries? c. What responses would promote **distributive justice**? d. What responses would preserve **human dignity**? e. What responses would promote the value of **human life**? f. What responses are **practical** given the resources available? g. What responses would protect **freedom**, both of the wrongdoer and of other members of society? h. What responses would be in **proportion** to the seriousness of the wrong or injury? i. What responses might satisfy the desire for **revenge**?	

LESSON 9

How Would You Respond to the Wrongs and Injuries Described in This Selection?

Purpose of Lesson

This lesson provides you with an opportunity to apply the intellectual tools you have learned to a situation involving fraud, a broken agreement, and theft. When you have completed the lesson, you should be able to evaluate, take, and defend positions on the issues of corrective justice it contains.

Terms to Know

fraud
grand theft

Critical Thinking Exercise
TAKING POSITIONS ON AN ISSUE
OF CORRECTIVE JUSTICE

As you read this selection:

- identify the wrongs or injuries that occurred

- use the chart from Lesson 8 to analyze the situation and develop a position on the proper responses

Complete this exercise by dividing into groups. Each group should be responsible for developing a position on the issues. Afterwards, each group should present and explain its position and respond to questions from members of the other groups.

Sly Mercury and Freddy Steele were famous rock-and-roll stars. They signed a contract with Leon Carter, a well-known rock concert promoter, to do a concert in Los Angeles, California. Carter agreed to pay Sly and Freddy a huge sum of money to make their appearances.

In expectation of a great success, Carter arranged for the concert to be held in a large stadium. He spent more than $20,000 to advertise the event on local television and radio. He hired many people to do such things as work the lights, maintain security, and serve food. He also made a deal with a record company to make a live album of the concert.

A month before the concert, Sly and Freddy were approached by another promoter—Don Richter. He claimed that he was trying to raise money to help the Bosnian refugees—a group of people who had been left homeless because of a violent civil war in their country. Richter wanted Sly and Freddy to appear at a special concert he had arranged in San Francisco. He told Sly and Freddy that their presence at the event would insure a sell-out crowd. The profits from the concert, Richter claimed, would be used to send food and medical supplies to the starving refugees. Unfortunately, the benefit concert was scheduled for the same day as Carter's concert in Los Angeles. There was no chance of either date being changed.

Sly and Freddy decided to break the agreement with Leon Carter in Los Angeles and appear instead at the Bosnian Refugee Concert. Both felt that the worthiness of the cause made appearing in San Francisco more important. When Sly and Freddy announced their decision, Carter was furious. He swore he would sue Richter for interfering with the agreement he made with Sly and Freddy. Carter knew his losses would be very high. Not only would he lose the profits from the concert and the album, but he had already paid for

What do you think would be the proper responses to the wrongs or injuries described?

use of the auditorium, the concert promotion, and the workers.

Three days after the concert in San Francisco, a bombshell hit the world of rock and roll. Don Richter's concert for the Bosnian refugees was a **fraud**—a scheme to cheat people out of money through lies or false pretenses. Richter and some of his associates were arrested at the airport trying to make off with the money from the concert. It was revealed that Richter had never intended to give the profits to the refugees. The story had been designed to get Sly and Freddy to perform at Richter's concert and to insure a big turnout. Richter was arrested on charges of **grand theft**—stealing valuable property or a large amount of money. And true to his word, Carter sued Richter for interfering with his agreement with Sly and Freddy.

At Richter's trial, the following facts came to light. Although Richter was once very successful, his career as a promoter was failing. He was deeply in debt. He was depressed and afraid that he couldn't support his wife and four children. In desperation, he had hit upon the concert scheme. Richter expressed his regret for what he had done. He offered to turn over what remained of the concert money to help the Bosnian refugees and to arrange another concert for their benefit.

What do *you* think?

1. What would be proper responses to the wrongs and injuries described in this story?

2. Are the responses you suggested designed to correct the wrongs and injuries?

3. Are the responses you suggested designed to prevent further wrongs or injuries?

Using the Lesson

1. Working with your teacher, invite a lawyer to class to discuss the facts in this imaginary case. Ask the lawyer what legal remedies would be available to the persons who were wronged and injured. Also, ask what punishment the person responsible for the wrongs and injuries might have to face in the criminal courts in your state. Finally, ask the lawyer to describe actual cases of which he or she might be aware in which similar wrongs and injuries have occurred.

2. Bring to class newspaper clippings of situations involving fraud and broken contracts. Be prepared to present and evaluate the decisions made in these situations.

3. Write an editorial about this fraud case. Your editorial should explain what you think would be a proper response and why.

LESSON 10

What Would Be the Proper Responses to the River Pollution Described in This Selection?

Purpose of Lesson

This lesson provides a final exercise asking you to use the intellectual tools you have studied in this unit. When you have completed the lesson, you should be able to use the chart on pages 209–210 to evaluate, take, and defend positions on issues of corrective justice.

Critical Thinking Exercise

TAKING POSITIONS ON AN ENVIRONMENTAL ISSUE

Work in small groups for this activity:

- Identify the wrongs and injuries caused by the chemical company

- Use the chart from Lesson 8, pages 209–210, to develop positions on what responses should be used to correct the wrongs and injuries and to prevent such problems from occurring again

When you have developed your positions, you may wish to role play a town council meeting during which each group makes a five-minute presentation of its position. One person from each group may be selected to serve as a member of the town council to conduct the hearing. Members of the town council may ask questions during presentations. After hearing all groups, the council should discuss the issue and develop and present its response.

James Creek

James Creek is a small town located in a beautiful valley. Much of the town's life is centered around its river. Fishing, boating, and swimming are among the townspeople's main pastimes. Tourists come from miles around to enjoy James Creek. The river also serves the town's economic interests. Located on its banks is the recently built Diamond Chemical Company plant.

Several years ago, Diamond's representatives came to James Creek scouting locations for a new

What would be the proper response to the river pollution described?

plant site. They were impressed with the town and its citizens and found a location on the river bank which would ideally suit their needs. Only when it came time to apply to the town council for a building permit did they run into a snag.

The town council was concerned about granting the application. They were worried about possible pollution. The members had heard of other towns that had their rivers spoiled because of pollution from chemical wastes. They did not want this to happen to James Creek.

After many meetings, the Diamond Chemical Company and the town government arrived at an agreement. It was decided that the city would grant the building permit, if Diamond promised to take full responsibility if the river became polluted. The company agreed to use the utmost care to prevent any pollution from entering the river. If at any time pollution was discovered, the town council could name a committee to investigate the situation and recommend a fair

response. The committee's recommendations would be binding on the town government and the Diamond Chemical Company. The Diamond Company agreed to these terms.

For two years everything went well. The plant was constructed and began to operate. New jobs became available for the townspeople and the economy boomed. Then, one spring, just before fishing season, thousands of dead fish were discovered floating in the river. Also, several children who swam in the river became ill. Soon the townspeople and tourists were afraid to use the river's recreational facilities.

Within several days, the town council had selected a committee to investigate the situation and to make recommendations. Experts testified that the river was polluted. Tests proved that a large quantity of poisonous chemicals had seeped into the river and had caused the damage. Further investigations showed that officials of Diamond Chemical Company had been warned of such a possibility by an engineer they had hired. Because costs of building the plant had been higher than expected, the officials had decided not to install the filter their own engineer had recommended. It was shown that this filter would have prevented pollution.

Before making their final recommendations, the members of the committee decided to hold a town meeting to hear damage claims. Many townspeople came to participate. Everyone wanted the river restored to its prior condition. Officials estimated it would cost $500,000 to clean up the river and another $50,000 to restore the fish population. Families whose children became ill demanded payment of medical expenses. Each of these families wanted $750 for doctor bills and another $1,000 apiece to compensate their children for their pain and suffering. Businesses that rented boats and supplied fishing equipment claimed that they had lost large amounts of money. They claimed boat rentals were down $75,000 from the previous year. Representatives from the chamber of commerce claimed that the whole town had suffered. They suggested that Diamond should be required to pay a heavy fine. They felt an example should be made of Diamond so that if any other company came to James Creek it would be warned in advance. Everyone agreed on one thing—nothing like this should ever happen again.

What do *you* think?

1. What responses to the wrongs or injuries described in the selection did your group recommend?

2. How might your group's responses correct the wrongs or injuries?

3. How might the suggested responses prevent or deter similar wrongs or injuries?

Using the Lesson

1. Invite a representative of a conservationist or environmental group to class to discuss actual cases similar to the one presented in this lesson. Ask the person what responses his or her group asks for in such situations.

2. Do research to find out what responses were made to one of the following environmental disasters, and report what you learn to the class:

   ■ Exxon Valdez oil spill in Alaska
   ■ Chernobyl nuclear power plant meltdown in Russia
   ■ Union-Carbide chemical plant explosion in Bhopal, India

3. Identify a problem of corrective justice in your school, community or state. Present a report to your class explaining the problem, how it involves corrective justice, and what other values and interests might be involved. Use the chart on pages 209–210 to develop a position on the issue, or explain why you are unable to develop a reasonable position on the basis of the facts available to you.

Unit Four: What Is Procedural Justice?

How do the situations illustrated in these pictures show issues of procedural justice?

Purpose of Unit

This unit deals with **procedural justice**, that is, with the **fairness** of **procedures** or ways of doing things. You will learn why procedural justice is important and the intellectual tools useful in evaluating, taking, and defending positions on issues of procedural justice.

When you have completed this unit you should be able to define procedural justice and explain its importance. You also should be able to use the intellectual tools in this unit to make thoughtful decisions about issues of procedural justice.

LESSON 11

What Is Procedural Justice?

Purpose of Lesson

This lesson introduces you to the subject of procedural justice. The lesson provides a definition of procedural justice and explains its importance.

When you have completed the lesson, you should be able to define procedural justice, explain its importance, and identify issues involving procedural justice from your own experience.

Terms to Know

procedural justice
due process of law
Bill of Rights

What are the purposes of procedural justice?

Procedural justice refers to the **fairness of the ways information is gathered and decisions are made.** It does **not** refer to the fairness of the decisions themselves.

The goals of procedural justice are

- to increase the chances of discovering information necessary to make wise and just decisions

- to insure the wise and fair use of the information in making decisions

- to protect important values and interests, such as the right to privacy, human dignity, freedom, distributive justice, and efficiency

Critical Thinking Exercise

EXAMINING ISSUES OF PROCEDURAL JUSTICE

Each of the following imaginary situations involves one or more issues of procedural justice. Read the situations and work with a study partner to answer the questions that follow them. Be prepared to share your answers with the class.

1. Two neighbors inform the police that you look very much like one of a group of teenagers who broke into the school over the weekend and destroyed property in several classrooms. The police arrest you and charge you with vandalism.

2. Your P.E. teacher decides to let the class choose what game they will play during the physical education period. The teacher asks for suggestions from several students and then says, "O.K., that's it—volleyball." Although you and several friends who wanted to play basketball raised your hands, you were not given an opportunity to make your suggestion before the decision was made.

3. Acting on a tip from an informer, the secret police broke into Alicia's house and searched for materials critical of the government. When they found several books by writers with "foreign" sounding names, they took Alicia to the police station. After being questioned for five days without sleep and with nothing to eat but bread and water, Alicia confessed. She admitted she had criticized the government several times. She was then tried as a traitor, convicted, and sent to a work camp for ten years.

Why might it be important to require that fair procedures be used to gather information?

4. A commission was established by the federal government to license industrial plants on public lands. The commission was required to hold public hearings before giving licenses. Several times, however, the commission refused to allow certain groups to make presentations at public hearings. The commission claimed that its staff had already studied and rejected the positions the groups wished to present.

What do *you* think?

1. What was the information gathered in each situation? What decision was to be made on the basis of the information?

2. How fair were the procedures used to gather the information or to make the decision in each situation? How could you make the procedures more fair?

Why is procedural justice important?

It is not unusual for people to ask, "Who cares about the way people get information or the way they make decisions, so long as they get the information they want and the decisions are good ones?" By the time you have finished studying this unit, you should understand the importance of procedural justice and be able to explain why people should care about the way information is gathered and the way decisions are made.

Scholars say that it is possible to tell how much value governments place on freedom, human dignity, and basic human rights by examining how carefully they provide for procedural justice in the actions of their police, courts, and other government agencies.

The importance placed on procedural justice by the Founders of our nation led them to include basic rules for procedural justice in the United States Constitution and in the **Bill of Rights** (the first ten amendments to the Constitution).

What do *you* think?

1. Why might the way information is gathered or the way a decision is made be important?

2. Give an example of the importance of using fair procedures at school or in your community.

Why are law enforcement agencies and the courts responsible for using fair procedures?

All societies have found it necessary to give certain officials the authority to gather information about suspected crimes and to arrest persons suspected of breaking laws. They also have found it necessary to give authority to certain

How does the right to trial by jury help guarantee a fair hearing for people accused of crimes? What other rights can you think of that help guarantee a fair hearing?

officials to hold hearings to decide whether or not a person is guilty of a crime or to settle conflicts among people. In the United States, these activities are usually carried out by persons working in our law enforcement agencies and our courts.

Because great power over human life and property is given to people working in agencies of government, a set of rules is needed to limit that power and say how it must be used. One set of these rules prohibits the government from taking a person's life, liberty or property without **due process of law**. In most situations this means that the government cannot act against a person without giving the person a fair hearing. Due process also requires law enforcement agencies to respect important values such as privacy, human dignity, and freedom when they gather information and arrest people.

The United States Constitution and Bill of Rights contain some of the rules of procedural justice that must be followed by law enforcement agencies

and courts. Other rules of procedural justice come from laws and regulations adopted by Congress, state legislatures, and other government agencies.

The Executive and Legislative Branches of Government

We often pay more attention to issues of procedural justice that arise from the activities of law enforcement agencies and the judicial branch than to those that may arise from the activities of other parts of our government. The reason for this attention may be that crimes and trials usually receive more publicity than the activities of other agencies of the executive branch or of the legislative branch of government.

It is important not to overlook the activities of the executive and legislative branches of government in our communities, states, and nation. These branches of government also have authority to gather information and make decisions that have a great effect on our everyday lives. For example,

Why should we be concerned about the procedures used by the executive and legislative branches of government?

they can draft citizens into military service, declare war, control trade, and collect taxes and decide how tax money will be spent.

The following lessons will introduce you to some intellectual tools useful in dealing with issues of procedural justice. You will use these tools to evaluate the fairness of procedures used in everyday life and by agencies of the executive, legislative, and judicial branches of government.

What do *you* think?

1. Review the goals of procedural justice. Why might it be important for all agencies of government to use procedures that further those goals?

2. Describe some procedures used by your student government or your school administration to gather information and make decisions. Explain why you think these procedures are fair or not.

Using the Lesson

1. Find examples of issues of procedural justice reported in the press or on television. Describe these issues to your class. Discuss the fairness of the procedures used to gather information and make decisions in these situations.

2. Read the Bill of Rights. Identify the provisions which deal with the procedures used by government to gather information and make decisions. How do these provisions ensure that people will receive a fair hearing? How do they ensure that important values such as privacy, human dignity, and freedom will be protected?

LESSON 12

How Can You Evaluate Procedures to Decide If They Are Fair?

Purpose of Lesson

This lesson reviews the goals of procedural justice and introduces you to three sets of intellectual tools useful in dealing with issues of procedural justice. When you have completed the lesson, you should be able to explain the usefulness of these tools. A fourth set of intellectual tools will be examined in the next lesson.

Terms to Know

comprehensiveness
notice
predictability
flexibility
reliability
impartiality
detection of error

What ideas are useful in examining issues of procedural justice?

As you learned in the last lesson, the basic goals of procedural justice are to

1. increase the chances that all reliable information necessary for making wise and fair decisions is gathered

2. ensure the wise and fair use of the information in making decisions

3. protect important values and interests

These basic goals can be used in deciding whether or not procedures are fair. The following intellectual tools will help you examine the procedures used to gather information and make decisions. In particular, these tools will help you evaluate how well the procedures serve the first two goals of procedural justice. In the next lesson you will learn another set of intellectual tools to use in evaluating how well procedures protect other important values and interests. Together, these tools will help you make thoughtful decisions about issues of procedural justice.

Critical Thinking Exercise
EXAMINING INTELLECTUAL TOOLS

This exercise may best be accomplished during a class discussion of the steps led by your teacher, or you may wish to examine the steps in small groups and then discuss your responses with the entire class.

Read each step in the procedure. Answer the questions in each step as they apply to the examples that are provided. Then discuss the usefulness of each step, and give examples of how it might apply to situations you have experienced or observed.

1. **Identify the purposes of the information-gathering procedures.**

   What information is being sought?

   Why is this information needed?

   - A policewoman driving past a bank heard an alarm and saw a person looking frightened leave the bank in a great hurry. She stopped the person and searched him.

   - A city council held public hearings before deciding what kinds of recreational facilities to build in a public park.

What information is sought at public hearings?

2. **Evaluate the procedures used to gather information.**

   Do the procedures ensure that all reliable information necessary for making a wise and just decision is gathered?

   To answer this question, the procedures should be evaluated in terms of the following considerations:

   a. **Comprehensiveness**

      Are the procedures **comprehensive** or complete? That is, do the procedures ensure that **all** information necessary to make a wise and just decision will be gathered from **all** interested persons?

      ■ Although Huck was given a trial for stealing stamps from the post office, he was not allowed to present his side of the story.

      ■ Often committees of Congress will hold hearings in Washington, D.C. on subjects they think might require new laws, such as medical care or new ways to make air travel safer. Interested people and groups can participate in these hearings only if they can travel to Washington, D.C., to make their presentations.

b. **Notice**

   Do the procedures provide adequate **notice** or warning of the **time** and the **reason** for the hearing to allow interested persons to prepare adequately?

   ■ Martha was notified of her trial the morning it was to begin.

   ■ When the City Council decided to hold a public hearing on a property tax issue, they advertised the hearing widely in the city for two months before it was held.

Why is it important to give adequate notice of a hearing?

c. **Effective Presentation**

   Do the procedures allow interested persons to **present effectively** the information they wish to have considered in the making of a decision?

   ■ Adam was not permitted to have a lawyer help him present his side of the story at his trial.

- People accused of crimes who do not have enough money to hire their own lawyers often are provided a public defender at taxpayers' expense. Public defenders sometimes have so many people to help they may have only ten to fifteen minutes to prepare for a hearing.

Why is it important to make sure people accused of crimes can effectively present the information they wish to have considered?

d. Predictability and Flexibility

Are the procedures sufficiently **predictable** (established in advance) and **flexible** (able to change or adapt) to promote justice?

- The procedures used in Alice's trial were made up as the trial proceeded.

- Although Sarah's name had been placed on the agenda to speak at a meeting of her community group, she was late to the meeting because she had a flat tire. She arrived just before the meeting was about to close. When she explained what had happened, the chairperson allowed her to speak to the group even though she had missed her place on the agenda.

e. Reliability

Do the procedures ensure that the information gathered is **reliable** or trustworthy?

- Raul was not allowed to cross-examine the witness who testified against him.

- An eyewitness was permitted to testify about what he saw when a bridge collapsed. However, he was not permitted to testify about the cause of the collapse because he did not have a college degree in architecture or structural engineering.

3. **Evaluate the procedures used to make a decision.**

Do the procedures ensure that the information gathered will be used wisely and fairly?

To answer this question, the procedures should be evaluated in terms of the following considerations:

a. Impartiality

Do the procedures ensure **impartiality**—lack of bias or prejudice—in the making of decisions?

- The judge at Nadia's trial was the brother-in-law of an important witness.

- In the past, it was common for judges to be paid from fines they imposed on people they had found guilty of breaking laws.

b. Public Observation

Do the procedures used allow interested members of the **public** to **observe** how information is being used in making decisions?

- Maria was arrested secretly in the middle of the night and was tried in the jail without a jury. No one in her village knew what was happening other than the judge, police, and the witness testifying against her.

Why is the right to a public trial important?

- The Sixth Amendment to the Constitution of the United States provides all persons accused of crimes the right to a public trial.

c. **Provision for the Detection and Correction of Errors**

Do the procedures allow interested persons to review what was done in order to **detect** (discover) and **correct errors**?

- Gary was executed immediately after he was convicted. He had no opportunity to appeal the decision in his case.

- No record was kept of a city council meeting during which it was decided that the applicant should be given a contract to build a new school.

What do *you* think?

1. Should members of government agencies be allowed to gather information about persons in any way they wish? Why or why not? What values and interests might be endangered?

2. How might the considerations of comprehensiveness, notice, effective presentation, predictability, flexibility, and reliability help you evaluate the fairness of information-gathering procedures?

3. How might the considerations of impartiality, public observation, and provision for detection and correction of errors help you evaluate the fairness of decision-making procedures?

Using the Lesson

1. Bring to class a news clipping which describes an issue of procedural justice. Explain how you could use the intellectual tools you have discussed in this lesson to resolve the issue described in the news clipping.

2. Invite an attorney to class to discuss how well the court system meets the goals of procedural justice. Use the intellectual tools you have learned to ask questions of the attorney.

3. Invite a representative of a local city council or school board to visit the class to discuss how well the council's or board's procedures meet the goals of procedural justice.

LESSON 13

What Other Values and Interests Should Be Considered in Deciding Whether Procedures Are Fair?

Purpose of Lesson

In this lesson you will examine the fourth set of intellectual tools to be used in dealing with issues of procedural justice. You will apply the tools you have studied in this unit to evaluate the procedures used in a historical case, "The Trial of Sir Walter Raleigh."

When you have completed this lesson, you should be able to use a chart containing all of the tools you have learned to develop and support positions on the fairness of procedures used in various situations.

Considering Related Values and Interests

The intellectual tools described in the previous lesson are useful. But they are not enough to enable you to decide if procedures are fair. For example, a procedure such as torture may be very effective in gathering information, but still be unfair because it violates important values such as human dignity. This lesson explains a fourth set of intellectual tools to use in examining issues of procedural justice. These tools will help you evaluate how well information-gathering and decision-making procedures protect important values and interests.

Critical Thinking Exercise
EXAMINING INTELLECTUAL TOOLS

This exercise may best be accomplished during a class discussion of the steps led by your teacher, or you may wish to examine the steps in small groups and then discuss your responses with the entire class.

Read each step in the procedure. Answer the questions in each step as they apply to the examples that are provided. Then discuss the usefulness of each step, and give examples of how it might apply to situations you have experienced or observed.

4. **Consider related values and interests.**

   Do the procedures protect related values and interests?

   To answer this question, consider:

   a. **Privacy and Freedom**

      Do the procedures violate the right to **privacy** or **freedom**?

      ■ The police suspected Jack of dealing in illegal drugs. In order to get a search warrant authorizing them to search Jack's house, they had to persuade a judge they would likely find illegal drugs there.

How does the requirement of a search warrant help protect our privacy?

■ After Huck was arrested for stealing stamps from the post office, he was kept in jail for two years before a trial was held to determine if he was guilty of breaking the law. He was not given an opportunity to to be set free on bail while waiting for his trial.

b. **Human Dignity**

Do the procedures violate basic ideas about the right of everyone to be treated with **dignity** no matter what his or her beliefs or actions may be?

■ In some countries torture is used to force people to reveal information and to confess to crimes. In the United States, the Fifth Amendment to the Constitution provides that no person can be forced to be a witness against himself in a criminal case.

■ During the early history of our country, people found guilty of certain crimes were covered with tar and feathers.

c. **Distributive Justice**

Do the procedures violate basic principles of **distributive justice**?

■ At a recent board of education meeting, all people who wanted to speak were given equal time on the agenda.

■ Earlier in our nation's history, only white males were permitted to vote and serve on juries.

d. **Practical Considerations**

Do the procedures satisfy reasonable **practical considerations**?

■ When Martin was tried for intentionally injuring another basketball player, he claimed the right to require all 5,000 people who attended the game to be witnesses at his trial.

■ After the defendant had interrupted the trial with several outbursts, the judge warned him he would be removed from the courtroom if he disrupted the trial again.

What do *you* think?

1. Why might it be important to consider the values of privacy, freedom, human dignity, and distributive justice in evaluating issues of procedural justice?

2. Why might it be important to take practical considerations into account in evaluating issues of procedural justice?

3. How might an effective way of gathering information violate important values and interests?

Critical Thinking Exercise
EVALUATING PROCEDURES IN A FAMOUS TRIAL

Read the following account of the arrest and trial of Sir Walter Raleigh. Work in small groups or with a study partner to complete the chart of intellectual tools on page 229. Be prepared to discuss your answers with the rest of the class.

The Trial of Sir Walter Raleigh

Sir Walter Raleigh was one of the most colorful figures in English history. Soldier, sailor, explorer, poet, statesman, scientist—Raleigh seemed to do well in almost everything he tried.

As a young man, Raleigh caught the attention of Queen Elizabeth I of England. She was impressed by his sharp wit, bold advice, and daring exploits. A fierce fighter and expert seaman, Raleigh rapidly became one of the Queen's favorites.

When Elizabeth died in 1603, James I became King of England. This gave Raleigh's enemies a chance to plot against him. They told the King that Raleigh had plotted with a man named Lord Cobham to overthrow him.

On the night of July 20, 1603, as Raleigh stood on the terrace of his home talking with friends, there was a loud knock at the door.

"In the name of his majesty, James I, open the door," someone shouted.

Walter Raleigh (1554–1618)

Suddenly the door was flung open and in walked Sir Robert Cecil, first secretary to the King and Raleigh's sworn enemy. With him were several members of the king's guard.

"In the King's name I place you under arrest," Cecil said.

"On what grounds?" Raleigh asked.

Cecil would not reply. Raleigh was taken away. His friends did not dare to protest.

Raleigh was questioned by Cecil in private. He had no chance to know the charges against him or to confront his accusers. He was not permitted the help of a lawyer. While being questioned, Raleigh learned that Cecil had tricked Lord Cobham into accusing Raleigh of treason. Cecil had accomplished this by telling Cobham that he had been accused of treason by Raleigh.

Raleigh knew there was little he could do if the King wanted him to be killed. Judges had been removed from office and juries had been put in jail for acquitting people the King wanted to keep in prison.

There was almost no evidence against Raleigh. Although he may have known something about the plot against the King, he had no part in it.

King James I of England (1556–1625)

Raleigh was brought to trial on November 17, 1603. The proceedings took place behind locked doors.

One of the judges at Raleigh's trial was Lord Thomas Howard, who had fought with Raleigh in the past and hated him. Another was Lord Henry Howard, who later admitted that he had actually started the plot against the king for which Raleigh was now being tried. Sir Robert Cecil, the man who had arrested Raleigh in the first place, was also one of the judges.

Raleigh had prepared himself as well as possible, but he was unable to present his defense effectively. He did not have the help of a lawyer or any other assistant. All Raleigh had was ink and paper to take notes. He could not speak until he was given permission to do so, and this permission was almost never given. Whenever Raleigh rose to protest a point in the prosecution's case against him, he was silenced immediately.

The "confessions" written by Lord Cobham were the most important evidence used against Raleigh. Raleigh asked that Lord Cobham be brought to court so that he could question him. Lord Cobham was alive and could have been brought to the trial. But the judges were afraid that Raleigh could prove his innocence if this were permitted. They refused to let Raleigh face his accuser.

The judges took just fifteen minutes to find Raleigh guilty. He was sentenced to be executed. However, on the day his sentence was to be carried out, Raleigh's punishment was reduced. He spent the next thirteen years as a prisoner in the Tower of London. Whenever Raleigh asked to speak with the King, in order to have his case reopened, his request was always denied.

What do *you* think?

1. Were the procedures used for gathering information and making a decision fair? Why or why not?

2. What suggestions would you make, if any, for improving the procedures used? Why?

Using the Lesson

1. Read the Bill of Rights. Identify the provisions that would have prevented the violations of procedural justice that occurred in the trial of Sir Walter Raleigh.

2. Watch television programs involving law-enforcement officers, private detectives, or courts. Evaluate the fairness of the procedures used by applying the intellectual tools you have studied.

3. Imagine you are Sir Walter Raleigh. Write a letter to the king explaining what steps in the procedure used in your trial were unfair and how they should be corrected.

Intellectual Tool Chart for Issues of Procedural Justice

Questions	Answers
1. What **information** is being sought? Why is this information needed?	
2. Do the procedures ensure that **all reliable information** necessary for making a wise and fair decision is gathered? Consider: a. comprehensiveness b. notice c. effective presentation d. predictability and flexibility e. reliability	
3. Do the procedures ensure that the information gathered will **be used wisely and fairly** in making a decision? Consider: a. impartiality b. public observation c. detection and correction of errors	
4. Do the procedures **protect important values** and interests? Consider: a. privacy and freedom b. human dignity c. distributive justice d. practical considerations	
5. Do you think the procedures adequately serve the goals of procedural justice? What changes (if any) would you make? Explain your position.	

LESSON 14

Were the Procedures Used in This Situation Fair?

Purpose of Lesson

This lesson provides an opportunity to use the intellectual tools you have studied to evaluate the fairness of the procedures used in a school discipline case. After reading the facts in the case, you will be asked to evaluate, take, and defend positions on the issues involved.

Critical Thinking Exercise
EVALUATING, TAKING, AND DEFENDING POSITIONS

Your class should be divided into small groups. As you read this selection, examine carefully the procedures used by the teacher and principal as they gathered information and made their decision. Be prepared to take a position on whether the procedures promoted the goals of procedural justice. Use the chart on page 229 to remind you of the intellectual tools to be considered.

Each group should present its position to the whole class for further discussion. This selection also may be used to role-play a court hearing. If your class decides to role-play a court hearing, use the procedures which follow the story.

The State Examination

Lilly Adams was a senior at Phillips High School in New York when she took the State Regents Examination on American History and World History in January. At the beginning of the three-hour examination period, each student was given two sheets of yellow scratch paper and the printed test. Near the end of the examination, a monitor noticed that Lilly was referring to a piece of scratch paper that had notes written on both sides.

He took the paper from Lilly and gave it to the teacher supervising the test. The teacher took Lilly and the piece of scratch paper to the principal.

Lilly explained to the principal that she had prepared the notes during the first half-hour of the examination period when the information was still fresh in her mind from studying for the exam. The principal asked Lilly to write and sign a statement explaining what she had done. He then continued to question Lilly for two hours. Later, the principal described what happened in these words:

"Since it seemed impossible for Lilly to have written the notes as she said she had in a half-hour at the beginning of the examination, I challenged her, not to do the same over again, but just to copy the notes she had written as fast as she could on the same kind of paper. In twenty minutes she was not able to copy one fourth of the notes. . . .

"I questioned Lilly again. She finally admitted she had cheated. I tore up the written statement she had signed and asked her to write a new statement telling what she had done. She wrote a new statement and finally signed a confession which read, 'I cheated.' All through this time Lilly was in a highly excited emotional state and in tears."

The next day, when she had calmed down, Lilly told the principal she wanted to take back her confession. The principal refused.

On January 31, the principal wrote a letter to the New York State Department of Education which said:

"I regret to report that Lilly Adams cheated on the State Regents Examination in American History and World History given this January. Her address is . . . ."

The State Department of Education then took away all of Lilly's privileges. She was identified as a cheater, given a zero on the test, and denied the right to take any future state examinations, including the state scholarship and college entry tests, until her privileges were restored.

The loss of her privileges also meant she was prevented from receiving an academic diploma for graduation from high school. An academic diploma is almost always required for admission to a college. Instead, she was given a general or nonacademic diploma. Lilly's privileges could be given back to her after a year if she had shown exemplary behavior and was recommended for reinstatement by the principal. Her record, however, would still show a zero on the examination which would mean that she had cheated. Many colleges would not accept a student with such a record.

In early February, Lilly's family hired a lawyer. He wrote a letter to the president of the Board of Education. He complained that Lilly had been punished without having been given a fair hearing. He said the procedures used by the principal and teacher to determine whether Lilly had cheated had not been fair.

In early March, the assistant superintendent of the school system wrote to Lilly's lawyer and suggested that a meeting be held with the school administrators, Lilly, her parents and her lawyer the next week. The assistant superintendent made it clear that the lawyer was invited only as an observer and would not be able to participate actively in the meeting in support of Lilly. The lawyer refused to accept this condition.

A hearing was eventually held by the school administrators to discuss the matter. Lilly, her parents, and her lawyer refused to attend. At the hearing the school administrators concluded that the principal had been correct and that Lilly had cheated.

What do *you* think?

1. Were the procedures used by the school officials fair? Why or why not?

2. What changes, if any, would you suggest for improving the procedures? Why?

3. What might be the advantages and disadvantages of the procedures you have suggested?

4. What values and interests would be promoted by your suggestions?

Procedures for a Moot Court Hearing

1. The class should be divided into three groups as follows:

   ■ Group 1 should develop a five-minute presentation supporting the position that the procedures used in the case were fair and reasonable.

   ■ Group 2 should take the position that the procedures were unfair and that the school officials should either dismiss the charges or give Lilly a new hearing.

   ■ Group 3 should serve as judges and conduct the hearing.

2. During a preparation period, Group 1 and Group 2 should develop their positions and prepare to respond to questions. Group 3 should prepare questions to ask the presenters from Group 1 and Group 2.

3. The hearing should be conducted by the judges, one of whom should be selected as chairperson. Each side may be given five minutes for its prepared statement and five minutes to answer questions from the judges.

4. After both sides have had an opportunity to be heard, the judges should discuss which arguments they found to be most persuasive and decide whether to rule in favor of Lilly or in favor of the school officials. The judges should explain their decision to the class.

Using the Lesson

1. Working with your teacher, visit a court and observe the procedures used. If your teacher is able to arrange it, speak with the judge during a break in the hearing. Ask the judge to explain how the procedures you have observed are designed to meet the goals of procedural justice.

2. Working with your teacher, invite a person to class who is knowledgeable about administrative hearings, mediation proceedings, and/or arbitration hearings. Ask the person why such hearings are used, how they meet the goals of procedural justice, and what other values and interests they may serve.

3. Imagine you are a judge. Having heard the arguments in the Lilly Adams case, write a one or two page opinion stating your views as to whether procedural justice has been denied. Your opinion should explain the reasons for your views. It also should include any recommendations you would make for improving the procedures.

LESSON 15

Were the Procedures Used in This Administrative Hearing Fair?

Purpose of Lesson

This lesson provides a final exercise in applying the intellectual tools you have studied in this unit. You will evaluate the procedures used by a federal commission to investigate issues involving civil rights, and role-play a Congressional hearing on whether to change the procedures. When you have completed this lesson, you should be able to use these intellectual tools to evaluate, take, and defend positions on the fairness of procedures used by the commission to conduct its investigations.

Voter registration efforts in Atlanta, Georgia (1963)

Terms to Know

civil rights
registrar

Critical Thinking Exercise
EVALUATING, TAKING, AND DEFENDING POSITIONS

In this exercise your class will role-play a Congressional hearing. As you read this selection, pay close attention to the procedures used by the Civil Rights Commission in gathering information to report to Congress and the president. Be prepared to take a position on which procedures used by the Commission promoted the goals of procedural justice and which did not. Then use the procedures which follow the story to conduct the role-play exercise.

The Civil Rights Commission

The United States Commission on Civil Rights is a part of the executive branch of the federal government. It is responsible for gathering information on various issues involving **civil rights**—the rights of people to be treated fairly by and to participate in their government. The commission reports the information it gathers to the president and Congress. The main purpose of the commission is to investigate and find facts. It is not a court, it does not hold trials, and it does not punish people for breaking laws.

In conducting its investigations, the commission has the right to require people to come before it and testify. When it requires a person to testify, the commission does not have to inform the person

■ what it is investigating

■ whether there are any charges against the person, or what the charges might be

■ who may have filed a complaint against the person

What arguments can you make to support your group's position?

The commission also does not have to give the person

- the right to cross-examine anyone who may have filed a complaint against the person

- the right to bring witnesses to the hearing

Typically, hearings of the commission are held in public, and they are often covered by the news media. If members of the commission decide that the evidence or testimony being heard might harm a person's reputation or be incriminating, the commission can decide to listen to the person's testimony in secret.

The civil rights issues investigated by the commission include situations in which it is claimed that someone has been unfairly deprived of his or her right to vote. In the late 1950s, a number of people in Louisiana who worked as **registrars**—registering people to vote—were accused of depriving African American citizens of the right to register to vote. Thus, they were accused of violating the citizens' civil rights under the Constitution of the United States.

A number of these registrars were required to testify before the Commission on Civil Rights. The registrars claimed that the procedures used by the commission were unfair. They said that

conducting the hearings in public might damage their reputations and cause them to lose their jobs. They also said their testimony might lead to criminal charges being brought against them. They claimed they had a constitutional right

- to know before they testified if they had been accused of depriving people of their rights

- to know who had accused them

- to require their accusers to be at the hearing and be subject to cross-examination

- to have other witnesses of their choice come to the hearing and be questioned

What do *you* think?

1. Were the procedures used by the commission fair? Why or why not?

2. What changes, if any, would you make to improve the procedures? Why?

3. What might be the advantages and disadvantages of the procedures you have suggested?

4. What values and interests influence your suggestions?

Procedures for a Congressional Hearing

1. The class should be divided into five groups as follows:

   ■ Group 1 will represent the commission. Develop a three-minute presentation supporting the position that the procedures used by the commission are fair and reasonable.

   ■ Group 2 will represent the registrars. Develop a three-minute presentation taking the position that the procedures used by the commission were unfair and should be changed to comply with your demands.

   ■ Group 3 will respresent the N.A.A.C.P. Develop a three-minute presentation supporting the position that the procedures used by the commission are necessary for the commission to investigate civil rights violations effectively.

   ■ Group 4 will represent the registrars' union A.F.S.C.M.E. Develop a three-minute presentation taking the position that the commission can investigate effectively even if its procedures are changed to protect the rights of witnesses.

   ■ Group 5 will serve as members of Congress. Prepare questions to ask the presenters from each group.

2. During a preparation period, Groups 1 through 4 should develop their positions and prepare to respond to questions. Group 5 should prepare questions to ask the presenters.

3. The hearing should be conducted by the members of Congress, one of whom should be selected as chairperson. Each side may be given three minutes for its prepared statement and three minutes to answer questions from the members of Congress.

4. After all sides have had an opportunity to be heard, the members of Congress should discuss whether to change the procedures used by the commission, and if so, how. The members of Congress should explain their reasoning to the class. The class as a whole may then vote on what the commission's procedures should be.

Using the Lesson

1. Look through newspapers or news-magazines, or watch television news or entertainment programs dealing with law enforcement or the activities of other agencies of government. Identify issues of procedural justice these sources contain. Be prepared to report your findings to the class and to discuss with them the fairness of the procedures you have observed.

2. Ask your teacher, counselor, or school administrator to describe the procedures used in your school system for gathering information and making decisions about students who may have broken school rules. Make a chart to illustrate the procedures. Be prepared to discuss the fairness of the procedures used with your class.

3. Arrange to visit and observe an agency of local government at work gathering information or making a decision. List the procedures used and be prepared to discuss their fairness with your class. For example, you might observe a court trial, a board of education hearing, a zoning commission hearing, or a city council hearing.

4. Write an editorial or draw a political cartoon about the procedural justice issues raised in the civil rights case you have studied in this lesson, or choose other procedural justice issues as your subject. Your editorial or cartoon should emphasize the problems that might occur if procedural justice is denied.

Concluding Exercise

What Issues of Justice
Does This Situation Raise?

When Mildred Penny was elected mayor she filled the most important positions in her city government with friends and relatives who had helped her get elected. Some of these people were well qualified for the jobs they were given and some were not. Other employees in city government as well as other citizens complained that they had not been given a fair opportunity to apply for several positions and that Mildred had used unfair procedures in selecting people to fill the positions.

A hearing was held to examine the complaints. The hearing committee was composed of three people appointed by Mildred, and two members of the community who had supported her election. After hearing the complaints, they decided that Mildred had the right to hire any people she wanted, and that none of the complaints required any further action or response by the city.

What do *you* think?

1. What issues does the situation raise in terms of

   - distributive justice
   - corrective justice
   - procedural justice

2. Do you agree or disagree with the way these issues were resolved? Explain your position.

3. How have the intellectual tools you have learned helped you to identify and make thoughtful decisions about issues of justice?

Conclusion

We hope that with the guidance of your teacher you have found this study of authority, privacy, responsibility, and justice to be useful and interesting. You have had the opportunity to develop the knowledge and skills you need to evaluate, take, and defend positions on issues that will arise in your day-to-day life. With the knowledge and skills you have aquired, you can assume an active and effective role as a citizen in a free society.

Picture Credits

Pages 2 and 170 (inset) — National Portrait Gallery

Front Cover, Pages iii, 11, 13, 17, 40, 41, 71, 97, 125, 132, 165, 213, 220, 227, 228, 237 — Library of Congress

Page 33 — Port Authority of N.Y. and N.J.

Page 47 — U.S. Supreme Court

Pages 48, 56, 67, 107, 109, 110, 116, 145, 178, 182, 198, 208, 233 — AP/Wide World Photo

Page 49 — Estate of Norman Rockwell

Pages 50 and 170 — National Archives